Salahddine Krit

Artificial Intelligence and Intellectual Property:

Salahddine Krit

Artificial Intelligence and Intellectual Property:

An Emerging Framework and Legal Challenges

ScienciaScripts

Imprint
Any brand names and product names mentioned in this book are subject to trademark, brand or patent protection and are trademarks or registered trademarks of their respective holders. The use of brand names, product names, common names, trade names, product descriptions etc. even without a particular marking in this work is in no way to be construed to mean that such names may be regarded as unrestricted in respect of trademark and brand protection legislation and could thus be used by anyone.

Cover image: www.ingimage.com

This book is a translation from the original published under ISBN 978-3-330-79877-9.

Publisher:
Sciencia Scripts
is a trademark of
Dodo Books Indian Ocean Ltd. and OmniScriptum S.R.L publishing group

120 High Road, East Finchley, London, N2 9ED, United Kingdom
Str. Armeneasca 28/1, office 1, Chisinau MD-2012, Republic of Moldova, Europe
Managing Directors: Ieva Konstantinova, Victoria Ursu
info@omniscriptum.com

Printed at: see last page
ISBN: 978-620-8-64449-9

INTRODUCTION TO ARTIFICIAL INTELLIGENCE

AND INTELLECTUAL PROPERTY

Dr. Salahddine Krit

TABLE OF CONTENTS

INTRODUCTION 3

CHAPTER 1: HISTORY AND EVOLUTION, THE ORIGINS OF ARTIFICIAL INTELLIGENCE 10

CHAPTER 2: FUNDAMENTAL PRINCIPLES 20

CHAPTER 3: TECHNIQUES AND METHODS 26

CHAPTER 4: PRACTICAL APPLICATIONS OF IA 32

CHAPTER 5: ETHICS AND CHALLENGES 38

CHAPTER 6: PROGRAMMING LANGUAGES 44

CHAPTER 7: TOOLS AND PLATFORMS 49

CHAPTER 8: ROBOTICS AND IA 56

CHAPTER 9: NATURAL LANGUAGE PROCESSING 62

CHAPTER 10: IA AND BIG DATA 68

CHAPTER 11: RECOMMENDATION SYSTEMS 74

CHAPTER 12: SAFETY AND IA 79

CHAPTER 13: IA IN VIDEO GAMES 83

CHAPTER 14: IA AND THE ENVIRONMENT 88

CHAPTER 15: THE FUTURE OF ARTIFICIAL INTELLIGENCE 94

CHAPTER 16: INTELLECTUAL PROPERTY 100

GENERAL CONCLUSION 106

REFERENCES 110

INTRODUCTION

Artificial Intelligence (AI) and Intellectual Property (IP) are two rapidly evolving fields that interact in complex and significant ways. This paper explores the legal, ethical and economic implications of this interaction, while highlighting the challenges and opportunities it presents. Through in-depth analysis, we highlight the need to adapt existing legal frameworks to meet the realities of a world where AI is redefining notions of innovation and creativity.

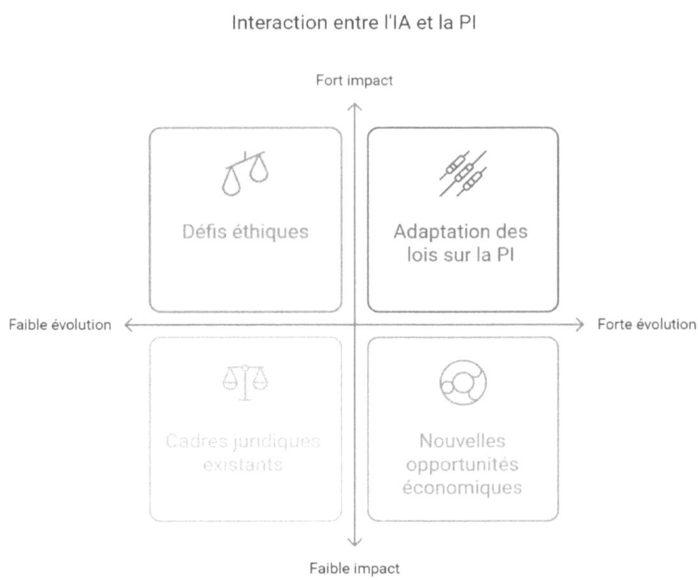

Link between AI and IP

To better understand the issues, we can explore the following sub-themes:

1. Legal implications of AI for intellectual property

Integrating AI into creative and innovation processes poses significant legal challenges. Here are the main issues:

- **Authorship**: When an AI generates a work, who is the author? For example, can music or a painting generated by an AI be protected? Under current legal regimes, only a natural person can be recognized as the author. However, some jurisdictions are considering adaptations to include "AI-assisted" works.

- **Ownership of rights**: If a company uses an AI developed by a third party to create an innovative product, who owns the rights: the company or the AI developer? Algorithm licensing and use agreements are often at the heart of this debate.

- **Respecting existing rights**: Can AI use protected works to train its models? For example, the use of copyrighted images or text in training databases is often characterized as copyright infringement, although some argue in favor of the "fair use" exception.

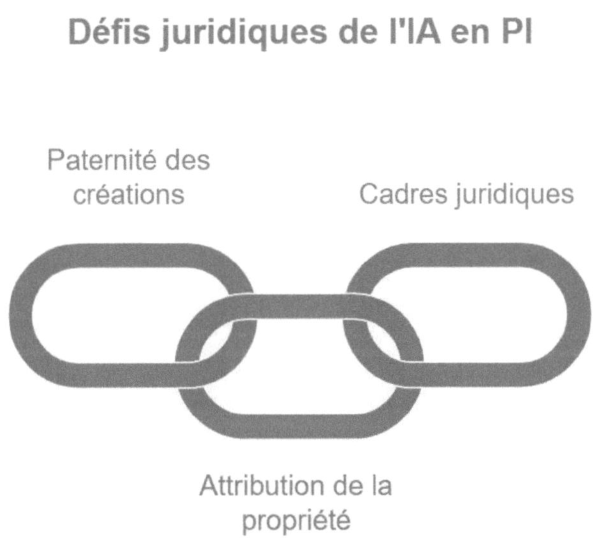

2. Concrete examples of interaction between AI and IP

- **Musical creation**: AIs like AIVA (Artificial Intelligence Virtual Artist) generate musical compositions. In 2020, music composed by an AI was registered under copyright in the user's name, sparking debate on the legitimacy of this protection.

- **Innovative patents**: AI algorithms are helping to design patentable products in fields such as pharmaceuticals and aerospace. However, some patent applications, attributed to machines as inventors, have been rejected by intellectual property offices such as the European Patent Office.

- **Generative art**: platforms like DALL-E or MidJourney produce illustrations using existing data. This raises questions about the potential infringement of original artists' copyrights.

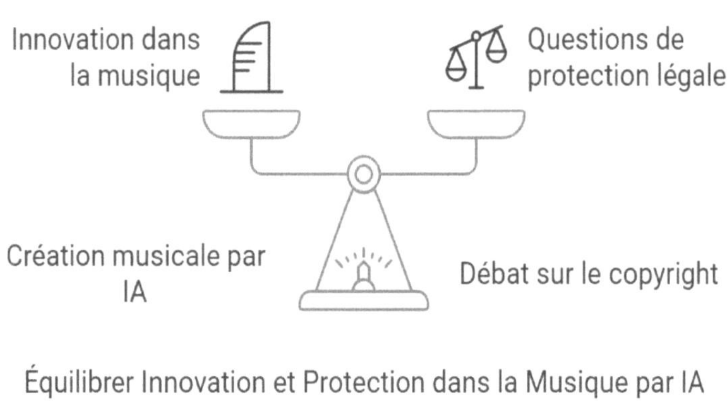

3. The role of AI in the management and enforcement of IP rights

AI can also play a crucial role in managing and protecting IP rights:

- **Infringement detection**: AI systems can analyze millions of online contents to spot copyright or trademark infringements. This is particularly useful for sectors such as music and film.
- **Predictive analysis**: AI tools can be used to assess the chances of success of IP-related litigation by analyzing past court decisions.
- **Process automation**: Platforms such as Copyright Office online use algorithms to speed up the registration of protected works.

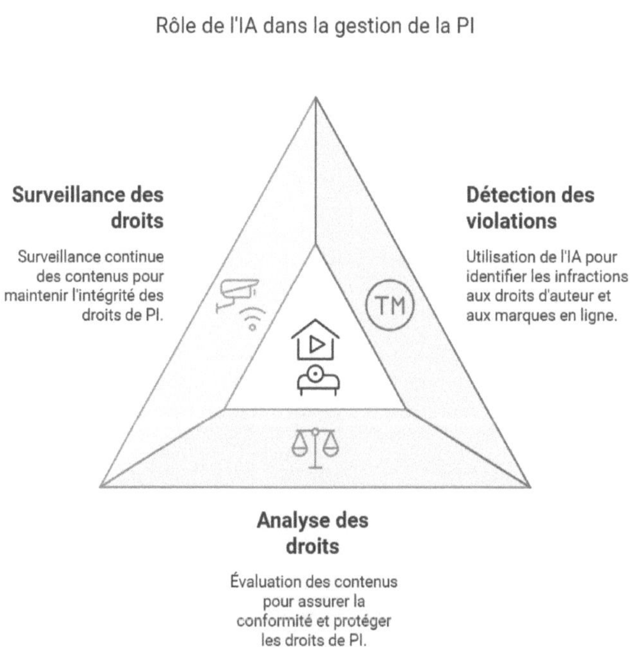

4. Ethical and economic challenges

- **The ethics of automated creativity**: Can AI be considered a creative entity, or is creation still the prerogative of humans?

- **Economic impact**: The automation of creative processes could disrupt entire industries, reducing the value of human work while increasing overall productivity.

5. Future prospects: Towards a suitable legal framework

To meet these challenges, several avenues are emerging:

- **Revising IP laws**: New legislation could officially recognize AI-generated works, clearly defining responsibilities.

- **Fair use and balance**: Include specific clauses to regulate the use of protected works in AI training databases.
- **International collaboration**: Given the global nature of technological innovations, harmonization of international laws is becoming essential.

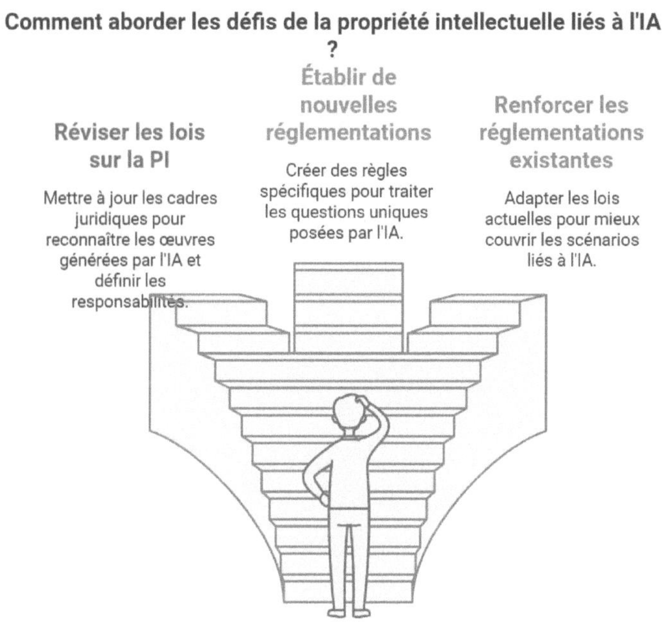

The interaction between artificial intelligence and intellectual property is redefining traditional concepts of creativity and innovation. While AI offers immense opportunities, it also poses unprecedented legal, ethical and economic challenges. An active dialogue between technology developers, lawyers and policy-makers is crucial to building a legal framework adapted to this new technological era.

CHAPTER 1: HISTORY AND EVOLUTION, THE ORIGINS OF ARTIFICIAL INTELLIGENCE

Introduction

Artificial Intelligence (AI) is a fascinating discipline that stems from the human aspiration to understand and reproduce our own cognitive abilities through machines. Since ancient times, this intellectual quest has been marked by spectacular advances, but also by periods of stagnation. This chapter traces the historical development of AI in detail, from its philosophical origins to its emergence as a modern scientific field. By exploring its roots, successes and setbacks, we will highlight how AI has gradually taken a central place in our contemporary society.

1.1 The first foundations : Ancient philosophy

The origins of artificial intelligence (AI) are deeply rooted in philosophical reflections on the nature of the human mind. This paper explores how ancient thinkers laid the foundations of logic and reasoning, influencing the future development of AI. Examining the contributions of Aristotle, as well as Eastern traditions and medieval thinking, we highlight early attempts to understand and reproduce human intelligence.

Aristotle's contributions

As far back as antiquity, thinkers such as Aristotle attempted to formulate theories to explain reasoning and logic. Formal logic, introduced by Aristotle, was one of the first systematic tools for structuring rational thought. His model of the syllogism - a form of deductive reasoning - formed a fundamental basis for future AI systems. By establishing rules for reasoning, Aristotle paved the way for a more systematic understanding of human thought.

Oriental Traditions

In the Eastern world, traditions such as Buddhism and Confucianism have also explored questions about the nature of mind and consciousness. These currents of thought, though different from Western approaches, have enriched the debate on what constitutes intelligence and the ability to reason. They introduced concepts of perception and cognition that continue to influence contemporary discussions on AI.

The Middle Ages and Automata

The Middle Ages were marked by studies on mechanics and automata, foreshadowing an attempt to replicate human behavior by artificial means. The erudition of thinkers such as Avicenna and Thomas Aquinas laid the conceptual foundations for envisaging a form of artificial intelligence, even if these ideas were still rooted in religious and philosophical paradigms. These reflections made it possible to anticipate future technological developments and imagine a world where the machine could imitate the human intellect.

The early foundations of artificial intelligence are inseparable from philosophical reflections on the mind and reasoning. Thinkers like Aristotle, as well as Eastern traditions and medieval studies, helped shape our understanding of intelligence. These ideas continue to influence the development of AI today, underlining the importance of philosophy in the evolution of intelligent technologies.

1.2 Mechanical Machines of the Renaissance

The Renaissance was a pivotal period marked by an explosion of technical ingenuity and scientific curiosity. This document explores the contributions of the inventors of this era, notably Leonardo da Vinci, and examines how their mechanical creations not only entertained, but also raised profound questions about the nature of life and mechanics.

Leonardo da Vinci's ingenuity

Leonardo da Vinci, one of the most brilliant minds of the Renaissance, designed a multitude of mechanical machines. His sketches of automata, such as the mechanical knight, are fascinating examples of how he attempted to simulate human actions. Although these inventions often remained on paper, they bear witness to an avant-garde vision that prefigured modern concepts of artificial intelligence.

Complex Clocks and Musical Automata

The Renaissance also saw the emergence of complex clocks and musical automata, which were primarily intended for entertainment. These creations were the fruit of advanced engineering, combining precision and aesthetics. Watchmakers and craftsmen of the time vied with each other in ingenuity to create mechanisms that not only measured time, but also offered fascinating spectacles.

Fundamental Questions about Mechanics and Life

The mechanical machines of the Renaissance gave rise to profound reflections on the difference between the mechanical and the living. Automata, though inanimate constructs, raised questions about the nature of intelligence and consciousness. These questions laid the foundations for philosophical discussions that continue to be relevant today, in the age of artificial intelligence and robotics.

In short, the mechanical machines of the Renaissance represent a period of unprecedented innovation that not only entertained, but also paved the way for reflections on the nature of humanity and technology. The work of iconic figures such as Leonardo da Vinci continues to inspire and provoke debate on the relationship between the living and the mechanical.

1.3 The Enlightenment and the first cognitive models

This article explores the contributions of the Enlightenment to the understanding of the human mind and early cognitive models, as well as the emergence of modern artificial intelligence in the 20th century. By examining philosophers' ideas and technological advances, we highlight the foundations that led to the creation of AI as a scientific discipline.

1.3 The Enlightenment and the first cognitive models

The 18th century brought important developments in the understanding of the human mind. Philosophers such as Descartes and Hobbes contributed to the idea that the mind could be understood as a machine, which influenced the creation of mechanical models of cognitive functioning. The Enlightenment saw scientists and scholars like Vaucanson design automata capable of reproducing complex behaviors, such as playing music or writing. These machines, though artificial, were seen as an attempt to reproduce human life in an artificial way.

The advent of computer science in the 20th century was a pivotal moment in the evolution of artificial intelligence (AI). This paper explores the major contributions of Alan Turing and the Dartmouth Conference, both of which played a crucial role in shaping AI as a scientific discipline.

The modern era of AI has been profoundly influenced by the work of Alan Turing, often regarded as the father of computer science. Turing raised fundamental questions about the ability of machines to think, laying the foundations for thinking about artificial intelligence. His famous Turing test, proposed in 1950, remains an emblematic criterion for assessing the intelligence of machines, based on their ability to imitate human behavior.

In 1956, the Dartmouth Conference marked a decisive turning point in the history of AI. Organized by pioneers such as John McCarthy, Marvin Minsky, Nathaniel Rochester and Claude Shannon, this event officially gave birth to AI as a scientific discipline. The researchers present explored innovative concepts such as formal logic, problem solving and the simulation of human intelligence by computers. It was at this conference that the term "artificial intelligence" was introduced, establishing a framework for future research in this field.

The Dartmouth conference not only catalyzed interest in AI, but also brought together brilliant minds around a common vision: to create machines capable of thinking and learning. This meeting paved the way for significant advances and laid the foundations for future developments in artificial intelligence.

This paper explores the early successes and limitations of artificial intelligence (AI) between 1960 and 1970, a pivotal period that saw significant advances in the field, while highlighting the challenges that led to periods of stagnation. The achievements of this era laid the foundations for modern AI, but the obstacles encountered also shaped future research.

Notable progress

The years following the 1956 Dartmouth Conference saw significant developments in the creation of AI systems. One of the most emblematic examples is the Logic Theorist program, designed by Allen Newell and Herbert Simon. This program demonstrated the ability of machines to solve complex problems by proving mathematical theorems, which was considered a major breakthrough in the field of AI.

Obvious limitations

Despite these successes, the limitations of AI systems at the time were quickly apparent. The programs, while impressive in their computational capabilities, lacked a contextual or intuitive understanding of problems. This led to growing criticism from researchers and practitioners alike, who began to question the viability of AI approaches based solely on logical algorithms.

AI winters

The high expectations raised by early successes also had negative consequences. When AI systems failed to live up to expectations, this led to periods of stagnation, often referred to as "AI winters". These periods were characterized by a withdrawal of funding and a slowdown in research, highlighting the need for a more nuanced and diverse approach to the development of artificial intelligence.

In conclusion, the period from 1960 to 1970 was marked by significant advances in the field of artificial intelligence, but also by limitations that led to critical reflections on the direction of research. These experiences were essential in shaping the future direction of AI.

Artificial intelligence (AI) has had its ups and downs throughout its history, but advances in machine learning in the 1980s and 1990s laid the foundations for a renaissance in the early 21st century. This article explores how algorithms such as backpropagation have made it possible to exploit artificial neural networks, and how the rise of deep learning has transformed a variety of sectors thanks to increased computing power and access to vast datasets.

The advances of the 1980s and 1990s

Despite the initial disappointments that marked the early days of AI, the 1980s and 1990s witnessed significant progress, particularly in the field of machine learning. One of the major developments was the backpropagation algorithm, which improved the training of artificial neural networks. Inspired by the workings of the human brain, these networks have begun to demonstrate their potential in complex tasks.

The rise of deep learning

With the advent of the 21st century, AI has undergone a veritable renaissance. The exponential increase in computing power, coupled with access to massive volumes of data, paved the way for the emergence of deep learning. This approach, based on complex neural network architectures, has revolutionized fields such as :

- **Computer vision**: Deep learning systems have enabled spectacular advances in image recognition and object detection.
- **Speech recognition**: advances in this field have made voice assistants more precise and efficient.
- **Natural language processing**: Deep learning has also transformed the way machines understand and generate human language.

The AI renaissance, fueled by machine and deep learning, has not only redefined the capabilities of machines, but also opened up new vistas for the future. Technological advances continue to evolve, promising even more impressive innovations in the years to come.

1.7 Modern AI and its societal impact

Artificial intelligence (AI) has become an inescapable part of our daily lives, transforming the way we interact with the world. This article explores the diverse applications of modern AI, while highlighting the ethical and societal challenges that arise. We'll examine the implications for employment, privacy and algorithmic bias, while highlighting the importance of a proper governance framework to navigate this new technological era.

The omnipresence of AI

Today, AI is integrated into many aspects of our lives. Voice assistants like Siri and Alexa make our daily tasks easier, while autonomous cars promise to revolutionize transportation. Recommendation algorithms, used by platforms like Netflix and Amazon, personalize our user experience according to our preferences. These technologies illustrate not only the spectacular capabilities of AI, but also its potential to transform entire industries.

Ethical and Social Challenges

Despite its advantages, the expansion of AI raises major concerns. One of the most pressing is the issue of employment. Automation could lead to the disappearance of some jobs, while others may require new, specialized skills. This raises the question of professional retraining and how to match education systems to market needs.

Another crucial challenge concerns privacy. AI systems collect and analyze huge amounts of personal data, raising concerns about security and privacy. Users need to be aware of how their data is being used and protected.

Finally, algorithmic biases represent a significant problem. AI systems can reproduce or even amplify existing biases, which can have harmful consequences, particularly in sensitive areas such as criminal justice or recruitment. It is essential to develop transparent and fair algorithms to avoid such abuses.

The Need for a Governance Framework

Faced with these challenges, it is imperative to establish a rigorous governance framework for AI. This includes creating regulations that protect the rights of individuals while fostering innovation. Governments, businesses and researchers must work together to develop ethical standards and responsible practices in the development and use of AI.

In conclusion, modern AI offers unprecedented opportunities, but it also poses significant challenges that require serious attention. By proactively addressing these issues, we can reap the benefits of AI while minimizing its societal risks.

Conclusion

The history of artificial intelligence is an epic made up of discoveries, revolutions and moments of questioning. By tracing its evolution, we gain a better understanding of the foundations on which this constantly evolving discipline rests. As AI continues to redefine the limits of what is possible, its future remains wide open, bringing opportunities and responsibilities for mankind.

CHAPTER 2: FUNDAMENTAL PRINCIPLES

In this chapter, we take a closer look at the key concepts that define and structure artificial intelligence (AI). We'll start with a clear definition of AI and then move on to explore basic algorithms, machine learning methods and their application in a variety of contexts.

2.1. Definition of AI

Artificial intelligence (AI) refers to the ability of machines to perform tasks that normally require human intelligence. These tasks include learning, reasoning, problem solving, perception and understanding natural language.

Simply put, AI is the field of scientific and technical research that aims to create systems capable of mimicking human cognitive functions. This is based on three key elements:

1. **Data**: Feeding systems information to learn. Data, which can be structured (such as tabular databases) or unstructured (such as images and text), is essential for training AI models.
   - Big data enables us to better understand trends and relationships.
   - Data pre-processing methods such as normalization and cleaning are often necessary to guarantee accurate results.
2. **Algorithms**: Algorithms are the mathematical and statistical programs that enable AI systems to extract meaningful information from data. For example, optimization algorithms adjust models to improve their accuracy.
   - Modern techniques such as deep learning depend on complex neural networks.

    - Conventional algorithms (decision trees, SVMs) are still widely used for simple problems or with limited data volumes.
3. **Computing power**: The rise of modern AI is largely due to the increased availability of graphics processing units (GPUs) and tensor processing units (TPUs), which enable complex calculations to be carried out rapidly. Cloud platforms also offer virtually unlimited capacity for training and deploying models.

AI can be classified into several categories, such as weak AI (specialized in specific tasks), strong AI (hypothetical and capable of replicating all human cognitive abilities), and general AI, which remains a future research goal.

2.2. Basic algorithms

Algorithms form the core of AI systems. They enable raw data to be processed, patterns to be detected, and predictions to be generated. Fundamental algorithms include :

a. Decision trees

Decision trees are tree models that use logical rules to classify or predict data. Each node represents a test on a variable, and each branch corresponds to a possible outcome. This type of model is intuitive and easy to interpret, making it popular in decision problems.

Common applications :

- Bank credit assessment.
- Medical diagnosis based on observed symptoms.
- Insurance risk analysis.

b. Neural networks

Inspired by human biology, artificial neural networks are made up of interconnected layers. These layers include :

- **Input layers**: Receive raw data.
- **Hidden layers**: Process data through calculations.
- **Output layers**: Generate predicted results.

Convolutional neural networks (CNNs) and recurrent neural networks (RNNs) are popular variants used for image and time series analysis respectively.

c. Support Vector Machines (SVM)

SVMs use hyperplanes to separate data into different classes. These models are particularly effective for classification problems with maximum margins between classes.

d. Clustering algorithms

These algorithms group data according to similarity, without the need for labels. Clustering includes methods such as k-means and DBSCAN. They are used for applications such as market segmentation and anomaly detection.

2.3. Different types of learning

a. Supervised learning

Supervised learning is based on the use of labeled data to train a model. The model learns to associate inputs with corresponding outputs. This approach is common for applications such as :

- **Image classification**: Identify objects or people in images.
- **Speech recognition**: Translate sounds into text.
- **Trend prediction**: Anticipate user demand or behavior.

Advanced techniques include :

- **Linear and logistic regression** for continuous and binary classification problems.
- **Model packages**, such as random forests and XGBoost, which improve accuracy by combining several models.

b. Unsupervised learning

Unlike supervised learning, this method does not use labeled outputs. The aim is to discover hidden structures in the data. Common applications include

- **Clustering**: Group together customers with similar behaviors.
- **Dimensionality reduction**: Make complex data sets more comprehensible.

c. Reinforcement learning

In this approach, an agent interacts with its environment and learns to maximize a cumulative reward. Each action can result in a positive reward or a penalty, prompting the agent to optimize its decisions. Applications include :

- **Video Games**: AI mastering games like Go and chess.
- **Robotics**: Teaching a robot to navigate in an environment.
- **Autonomous driving**: teaching vehicles to react optimally in different scenarios.

2.4 Importance of the Fundamental Principles

Mastering these basic principles is essential for understanding how AI systems work and evolve. They provide a solid foundation for developing applications tailored to current and future needs in a variety of fields, including healthcare, finance, education and transportation.

In summary, the fundamentals of AI, including its definitions, algorithms and learning methods, provide an overview of the capabilities and limitations of current technologies. These foundations serve not only to understand AI, but also to lay the groundwork for future innovations in this fascinating field.

CHAPTER 3: TECHNIQUES AND METHODS

In this chapter, we examine a range of fundamental techniques and methods that underpin the development of artificial intelligence (AI) and machine learning. These tools play an essential role in the creation of intelligent, adaptive systems capable of solving complex problems. We explore neural networks, genetic algorithms, fuzzy logic, expert systems and computer vision. Each of these sections is elaborated to provide in-depth details, practical examples, and key applications.

3.1 Neural networks

Artificial neural networks (ANNs) are computational models inspired by the functioning of biological neurons in the human brain. These models are made up of several layers of interconnected neurons, enabling them to process complex information and learn from data. The power of ANNs lies in their ability to generalize knowledge from examples.

Structure and operation

A typical neural network includes :

- **Input layer**: Represents raw data (e.g. pixels for images, words for text).
- **Hidden layers**: Perform intermediate transformations using non-linear activations such as ReLU (Rectified Linear Unit) or tanh.
- **The output layer**: Produces the final results, such as a probability for each class in a classification problem.

Each connection between two neurons is associated with a weight, adjusted during the entrainment process using an algorithm such as gradient descent. ANNs are often trained by minimizing a loss function that measures the difference between predictions and actual values.

RNA applications

1. **Image recognition**: CNNs (Convolutional Neural Networks) excel in tasks such as object identification and image classification. Algorithms such as ResNet or Inception, for example, are widely used in computer vision.
2. **Machine translation**: Models like Transformers (e.g. BERT or GPT) have revolutionized natural language processing (NLP), enabling precise, context-sensitive translations.
3. **Time series prediction**: in the financial or meteorological fields, RNAs such as RNN (Recurrent Neural Networks) or LSTM (Long Short-Term Memory) can be used to analyze past trends and predict the future.

Advantages and limitations

- **Benefits**: Ability to process unstructured data, adaptability to a variety of problems, exceptional performance for large data volumes.
- **Limitations**: Need for large amounts of data to train, high computational costs, opacity of models (black box).

3.2. Genetic algorithms

Genetic algorithms (GAs) are optimization and search methods inspired by the process of natural selection. They rely on evolutionary mechanisms such as mutation, crossover and selection to produce efficient solutions to complex problems.

How genetic algorithms work

1. **Initialization**: Creation of an initial population of potential solutions (individuals).
2. **Evaluation**: Each individual is evaluated according to a fitness function that measures his or her performance.
3. **Selection**: The best-adapted individuals are selected for reproduction.
4. **Cross-breeding and mutation**: Selected individuals produce a new generation by combining and altering their characteristics.
5. **Repetition**: The process is repeated until an optimum solution or a predefined stopping criterion is reached.

Applications

1. **Planning and scheduling**: optimizing schedules at airports or in industry.
2. **System design**: Automation of electronic circuit design or optimization of mechanical structures.
3. **Artificial intelligence for games**: Creating adaptive strategies in complex game environments.

Strengths and limitations

- **Strengths**: Ability to escape local minima, adaptability to a variety of problems.
- **Limitations** : Long calculation times, complex parameters (population size, mutation rate, etc.).

3.3. Fuzzy logic

Fuzzy logic can be used to process imprecise or ambiguous information by assigning degrees of truth to statements. Unlike traditional Boolean logic (true or false), it works with intermediate values, better reflecting the uncertainties of the real world.

Key concepts

- **Fuzzy variables**: Represent imprecise concepts such as "hot" or "cold".
- **Membership functions**: Determine the degree to which a value belongs to a fuzzy category.
- **Fuzzy rules**: deduce conclusions from fuzzy information ("If X is high and Y is low, then Z is moderate").

Applications

1. **Control systems**: Optimization of automatic braking systems in cars.
2. **Energy management**: intelligent control of HVAC systems.
3. **Decision-making**: Risk assessment in insurance and finance.

3.4. Expert systems

Expert systems are computer programs that reproduce the skills and knowledge of a human expert in a specific domain. They rely on a knowledge base and an inference engine to solve problems or recommend solutions.

Structure of an expert system

1. **Knowledge base**: Contains facts and rules relating to a domain.
2. **Inference engine**: uses algorithms to draw conclusions from available information.
3. **User interface**: Allows users to interact with the system.

Applications

1. **Medicine**: Diagnosis of complex diseases via systems like MYCIN.
2. **Finance**: Financial risk analysis and trend prediction.
3. **Engineering**: Computer-aided design (CAD) and technical troubleshooting.

3.5. Computer vision

Computer vision involves equipping machines with the ability to understand and interpret images and videos. This field relies on advanced image processing algorithms combined with deep learning.

Key techniques

- **Object detection**: Identify and locate objects in an image.
- **Image segmentation**: dividing an image into significant regions.
- **Deep learning**: CNNs (Convolutional Neural Networks) are at the heart of many advances in computer vision.

Applications

1. **Facial recognition**: securing electronic devices.
2. **Autonomous driving**: real-time analysis of the road environment.
3. **Health**: Early detection of disease from medical images.

Conclusion

In this chapter, we have explored key techniques and methods in artificial intelligence. Each approach, whether neural networks, genetic algorithms or expert systems, plays a crucial role in solving complex problems and improving intelligent systems. These tools form the foundations on which tomorrow's innovations are built.

CHAPTER 4: PRACTICAL APPLICATIONS OF IA

This chapter explores the diverse applications of artificial intelligence (AI) in several key sectors, including healthcare, finance, industry, transportation and education. AI is transforming these fields by improving efficiency, reducing costs and offering innovative solutions to contemporary challenges. Each section highlights concrete examples and the benefits associated with integrating AI.

4.1 AI in Healthcare

Artificial intelligence plays a crucial role in the healthcare sector, where it is used to improve diagnosis, treatment and patient management.

1. **Early diagnosis and precision**: Machine learning algorithms analyze complex medical data to detect diseases at an early stage, such as cancer or cardiovascular disease. For example, tools like DeepMind's AlphaFold predict protein structure, accelerating biomedical research. AI-based detection devices, such as medical image scanners, identify abnormalities with greater accuracy than human radiologists in some cases.
2. **Personalized treatments**: AI systems personalize treatments based on patients' genetic data and medical history, optimizing clinical outcomes. These approaches, known as predictive medicine and targeted therapies, reduce side effects and improve the overall effectiveness of care.
3. **Patient support**: Chatbots and virtual assistants, like Ada Health, provide 24/7 advice and reduce the burden on healthcare professionals. They also help monitor treatment compliance, by sending automated reminders or asking questions to assess the patient's state of health. These tools enable immediate and intuitive interaction, enhancing the overall patient experience.

4. **Cost reduction**: AI-based solutions help minimize costs in medical facilities, for example by automating administrative tasks such as booking appointments or processing medical invoices.
5. **Clinical research**: AI algorithms rapidly identify patterns in data, accelerating drug discovery and clinical trial design. They also reduce the time needed to validate a treatment's efficacy.

4.2 AI in Finance

In the financial sector, AI has become indispensable for guaranteeing security and improving efficiency.

1. **Fraud detection**: Systems such as Visa's use predictive models to analyze customer behavior and identify suspicious transactions in real time. These models integrate thousands of parameters, such as spending habits or geographical locations, to detect anomalies. The integration of AI makes it possible to react in milliseconds, which is crucial for blocking fraudulent activities before they cause significant losses.
2. **Robo-advisors**: These platforms, such as Betterment and Wealthfront, use algorithms to provide personalized investment advice, making wealth management accessible. These tools analyze user preferences, risk tolerance and market trends in real time to propose tailor-made portfolios.
3. **Trading optimization**: AI analyzes large volumes of data at unprecedented speed, enabling high-frequency trading and better decision-making. AI systems identify trading opportunities even before humans can detect them, offering a competitive advantage to the institutions that use them.

4. **Risk management**: AI enables risk to be assessed with greater precision, thanks to large-scale data analysis. These analyses help financial companies to anticipate economic crises and prepare strategies to deal with them.

4.3 AI in Industry

AI is transforming industry, ushering in a new era of automation and optimization.

1. **Predictive maintenance**: By analyzing sensor data, algorithms anticipate equipment breakdowns, reducing downtime and repair costs. This enables companies to reduce downtime and avoid considerable losses.
2. **Process automation**: Intelligent robots increase precision and efficiency on production lines. Tesla, for example, integrates AI systems into its factories to speed up production. This automation enables the industry to reduce human error while increasing production volumes.
3. **Supply chain optimization**: Platforms like Blue Yonder forecast demand and adjust stock levels, reducing waste. AI-based technologies help monitor freight transport, ensuring faster, more efficient deliveries.

4.4 AI in Transport

Transportation is being revolutionized by AI, from autonomous cars to traffic management systems.

1. **Autonomous vehicles**: Companies like Waymo and Tesla use deep learning algorithms to analyze sensor data, enabling cars to navigate

safely. These vehicles are designed to react to complex situations, making roads safer.

2. **Traffic management**: Intelligent systems optimize traffic flows, reducing congestion and improving road safety. AI helps forecast infrastructure needs and propose improvements based on data collected in real time.
3. **Sustainable transport**: AI applications, such as those from Uber Freight, reduce distances travelled empty, cutting carbon emissions. These systems can also optimize routes according to weather conditions or traffic forecasts.

4.5 AI in Education

Artificial intelligence is transforming the education sector by offering tailored, accessible solutions.

1. **Adaptive learning**: Platforms such as DreamBox and Smart Sparrow tailor content to students' individual needs, promoting a personalized experience. These systems rely on real-time analysis to identify weak points and adjust exercises.
2. **Task automation**: AI automates administrative tasks such as marking assessments, allowing teachers to concentrate on teaching. AI-based tools also improve scheduling and enrolment management.
3. **Learning support**: Educational chatbots, such as those integrated into Microsoft Teams, guide students and answer their questions in real time. These systems complement online courses and offer immediate support.

Conclusion

In conclusion, artificial intelligence is revolutionizing various sectors, bringing significant improvements in terms of efficiency, personalization and innovation. The practical applications of AI continue to evolve, promising a future in which these technologies will play an even more central role in our daily lives.

CHAPTER 5: ETHICS AND CHALLENGES

This chapter offers an in-depth exploration of the ethical issues and challenges associated with artificial intelligence (AI). By addressing the themes of privacy, bias, accountability, transparency and the impact on employment, we seek to demonstrate the importance of a rigorous ethical framework for the development and use of these technologies.

5.1 Ethical issues

AI ethics is an evolving field of study, focusing on how these technologies influence society. AI systems, by making automated decisions, have the capacity to alter life trajectories, redefine organizational processes and transform social relationships. This responsibility requires the establishment of ethical guidelines that balance technological innovation with the needs of humanity.

A central issue is to answer the fundamental question: how can we develop AI that respects human rights, promotes equality and avoids undesirable consequences? This question gives rise to debates on the priorities to be adopted, whether it's a question of prioritizing social justice, respect for privacy or the creation of economic value.

The ethical integration of AI into our society is based on key principles:

1. **Justice**: Ensuring that AI systems do not reinforce existing inequalities.
2. **Autonomy**: Respecting the ability of individuals to make informed decisions.
3. **Beneficence**: Maximizing benefits while minimizing risks.
4. **Non-maleficence**: Prevent AI from causing damage.
5. **Responsibility**: Ensure that decisions made by the AI can be explained and attributed.

Ethical dilemmas, however, are not easily resolved. For example, in the field of autonomous vehicles, who should take priority: the lives of passengers or pedestrians? These questions underline the need for extensive dialogue between stakeholders: developers, governments, users and civil society.

5.2 AI and privacy

Privacy is a major concern with the emergence of AI. As data-intensive technologies, AI systems raise crucial questions about the collection, analysis, storage and use of personal information. These practices entail major risks for individual rights and democracy.

One of the main difficulties is that users don't always understand how their data is collected or for what purposes it is used. For example, mobile apps, voice assistants and social networking platforms often exploit data for advertising targeting purposes, which can erode consumer trust.

Regulations such as the General Data Protection Regulation (GDPR) in Europe attempt to address these concerns. However, enforcement remains a challenge, not least because of the global reach of AI systems, which often extends beyond national jurisdictions.

AI-based systems must therefore adopt ethical approaches to guarantee privacy:

- **Data minimization**: Limit data collection to what is strictly necessary.
- **Anonemization**: Detach personal data from individual identifiers.
- **Informed consent**: Enabling users to understand the implications of using their data.

- **Proactive compliance**: Implement audits to verify compliance with data protection standards.

Ultimately, protecting privacy in the context of AI requires not only strict regulation, but also accountability on the part of developers and organizations.

5.3 AI biases

Biases are inherent in any AI system based on training data. They can be introduced by factors such as unrepresentative datasets or unconscious developer bias. These biases can produce discriminatory results, exacerbating social inequalities.

One well-documented example concerns facial recognition systems, which often have high error rates for individuals from ethnic minorities or genders under-represented in training data. This can lead to serious consequences, such as unjustified arrests or social exclusion.

To correct these biases, several strategies can be adopted:

1. **Data diversification**: Collect data representing a diverse range of users.
2. **Fair testing**: Develop methods for assessing the fairness of algorithms.
3. **Developer awareness**: Train technical teams to identify and eliminate bias.
4. **Independent audits**: Set up external reviews to verify the fairness of systems.

A proactive vision is needed to ensure that AI serves to reduce disparities rather than reinforce them.

5.4 Accountability and transparency

Accountability and transparency are closely linked to the societal acceptance of AI. These two principles help to strengthen public confidence in these technologies.

Responsibility implies that it is possible to clearly identify the actors responsible in the event of a malfunction or detrimental decision. For example, if an autonomous vehicle causes an accident, is it the fault of the manufacturer, the programmer, the user or some other factor? This question is still widely debated, and requires precise legal frameworks.

Transparency, meanwhile, aims to enable users to understand how AI systems work. This includes:

- **Explicability**: Provide clear explanations for decisions made by the AI.
- **Accessibility of information**: Make available documents describing the algorithms used.
- **Stakeholder engagement**: Include users in the design process to ensure that systems meet their needs.

These efforts are essential to ensure that AI systems respect societal values.

5.5 Impact on employment

AI is redefining the job market by automating tasks and creating new opportunities. However, these changes are not without consequences:

1. **Job losses**: Many sectors, such as manufacturing, transport and services, are seeing job losses.

2. **Job creation**: The emergence of new roles, such as AI ethics specialist, data analyst or algorithm developer, offers opportunities for skilled workers.
3. **Retraining**: Workers need to acquire new skills to stay relevant.

Strategies to mitigate these impacts include :

- Invest in education and training.
- Foster collaboration between governments, companies and academic institutions to anticipate future needs.
- Introducing social protection policies adapted to the digital economy.

Conclusion

The ethical issues surrounding AI are both vast and complex. They require a collaborative, multidisciplinary approach to ensure that these technologies are developed and used ethically, responsibly and for the benefit of society as a whole.

CHAPTER 6: PROGRAMMING LANGUAGES

In this chapter, we'll explore various programming languages used in the field of artificial intelligence (AI). We'll look at Python, R, Java and C++, as well as emerging languages that are gaining popularity in AI application development. Each language has its own characteristics, advantages and disadvantages, which influence its use in different AI contexts.

6.1 Python for AI

Python is often considered the language of choice for the development of artificial intelligence applications. Its simple, readable syntax and extensive library of modules (such as TensorFlow, Keras and PyTorch) facilitate rapid prototyping and the development of complex algorithms. Python also excels in data manipulation, thanks to libraries such as Pandas and NumPy, which enable large volumes of data to be processed efficiently. In addition, tools like Jupyter Notebook enable developers and researchers to easily prototype and share their work in the form of interactive notebooks.

Python offers an ecosystem of powerful libraries for deep learning and machine learning. For example, TensorFlow and PyTorch are widely used in applications ranging from image recognition to text generation. Keras, a high-level API running on top of TensorFlow, simplifies rapid experimentation. Open source projects such as Scikit-learn provide a panoply of machine learning algorithms suitable for a variety of tasks such as classification, regression and clustering.

Python is also ideal for AI-based systems, as it enables easy integration with external tools such as databases or cloud services. For example, Google Cloud, AWS and Azure services offer Python APIs for rapid model deployment. Finally, the very active Python community is an invaluable resource for developers looking to learn, collaborate or solve complex problems.

6.2 R and its applications

R is mainly used for statistical analysis and data visualization, but it has also found its way into the field of AI, particularly for machine learning. With packages such as caret and randomForest, R enables researchers and analysts to manipulate data and create predictive models. These packages offer a simplified interface for a wide range of algorithms, saving time while guaranteeing reliable results.

R stands out for its advanced visualization capabilities. Libraries such as ggplot2 and lattice can be used to create customized, interactive graphs. These visualizations can be combined with analysis tools to explore data in depth and communicate complex results clearly. In addition, Shiny, a framework developed in R, enables the rapid creation of interactive web applications, facilitating the dissemination of analysis results to non-technical stakeholders.

In the context of machine learning, R also offers tools such as XGBoost, which is suitable for predictive modeling competitions, and specialized packages for time series and spatial analysis. Although R is less widely used than Python for production systems, it remains a preferred choice for exploratory analysis and model prototyping.

6.3 Java and AI

Java is an object-oriented programming language that is widely used in the development of enterprise applications. In the field of AI, Java is appreciated for its portability and robustness. Thanks to the Java Virtual

Machine (JVM), applications developed in Java can be run on a wide variety of platforms without modifying the source code. This feature is particularly useful for AI systems that need to be integrated into heterogeneous infrastructures.

Java has a number of powerful AI frameworks, including Deeplearning4j, which offers native support for deep learning and can leverage GPUs to speed up computations. Weka is another well-known library for machine learning, offering a user-friendly interface and a vast collection of ready-to-use algorithms. In addition, APIs such as those in the Apache ecosystem (e.g. Spark) enable massive data to be processed in a distributed way, a crucial feature for large-scale AI projects.

Java is also present in mobile development, notably via Android, where it enables AI algorithms to be integrated into mobile applications. This combination opens up unique opportunities for creating intelligent applications capable of operating offline while exploiting the device's local resources.

6.4 C++ in AI systems

C++ is a low-level language that offers precise control over system resources, making it ideal for applications requiring optimum performance. In the field of AI, C++ is often used to develop embedded systems and applications requiring fast execution, such as video games and robotics. Its proximity to hardware minimizes latency and optimizes intensive calculations.

Many machine learning and deep learning libraries, such as TensorFlow and Caffe, are written in C++ for performance reasons. These libraries also offer bindings to other languages, enabling developers to take advantage of C++ performance while working in a high-level environment. Critical systems, such as high-frequency trading platforms and automotive control systems, often use C++ to guarantee reliability and efficiency.

6.5 Emerging languages

With the rapid evolution of technology, new programming languages are emerging and gaining popularity in the AI field. Languages such as Julia, which is designed for scientific computing and data analysis, and Rust, which focuses on security and performance, are beginning to attract the attention of AI developers.

Julia stands out for its ability to combine the ease of use of high-level languages with the speed of low-level languages. It is particularly well suited to matrix calculations and complex simulations. Rust, on the other hand, is renowned for its secure memory management and resistance to common errors such as buffer overflows. These features make it an attractive choice for AI-critical applications where reliability and security are paramount.

Conclusion

In conclusion, the choice of programming language for the development of artificial intelligence applications depends on the specific needs of the project, the skills of the developers and the performance requirements. Each of the languages discussed in this chapter has its own advantages and disadvantages, and it is essential to evaluate them in relation to the project's objectives.

CHAPTER 7: TOOLS AND PLATFORMS

7.1 Introduction

Artificial intelligence (AI) has become a key driver of technological innovation in many sectors, including healthcare, finance, logistics and transportation. As AI continues to redefine industrial paradigms, understanding the tools and platforms that support its development is crucial. These technologies are not only gas pedals of innovation, but also serve as catalysts for the adoption of advanced solutions by businesses and organizations of all sizes. This chapter explores these tools in depth, their historical evolution, selection criteria, and a case study illustrating their use in a real-life context. We will highlight how AI tools enable complex problems to be solved, while making innovation accessible to a wider range of professionals.

7.2 Importance of AI development tools

AI tools and platforms play a central role in simplifying complex tasks and enabling teams to focus on the creative and strategic aspects of their projects. Their importance can be broken down into several key dimensions: automation, accessibility, collaboration, and innovation.

Automating complex tasks

AI tools can automate many development stages, reducing technical barriers. For example:

- **Data preparation**: Libraries like Pandas and NumPy enable efficient data manipulation, while tools like TensorFlow Data Validation automate anomaly detection and data normalization.
- **Model design**: TensorFlow and PyTorch provide building blocks for creating complex architectures without having to reinvent the wheel.

- **Training and validation**: Platforms like AWS SageMaker offer pre-defined environments for training, validating and deploying models, eliminating the need to manually manage underlying infrastructures.

7.3 Accessibility for all skill levels

Historically, AI was reserved for experts in computer science or advanced mathematics. Today, thanks to intuitive user interfaces and well-documented libraries, even beginners can get started:

- **AutoML**: Tools like Google AutoML automatically generate high-performance templates without writing a single line of code.
- **Low-code platforms**: Solutions like DataRobot or H2O.ai offer drag-and-drop environments for designing and deploying AI models.

Collaboration and community

AI tools benefit greatly from active communities that foster knowledge sharing and open innovation:

- **Educational resources**: forums like Stack Overflow and platforms like GitHub are packed with tutorials, code examples and solutions to common problems.
- **Open ecosystems**: Open-source libraries, such as Scikit-learn or Hugging Face, enable everyone to contribute to the improvement of tools.

Accelerating innovation

With these tools, companies can rapidly prototype ideas and test their feasibility before investing in large-scale deployment. Ambitious projects, such as disease prediction or supply chain optimization, become accessible thanks to these innovations.

Historical overview and development

The field of AI tools has evolved dramatically, from rudimentary approaches to complex, sophisticated ecosystems. This section traces the history of AI tools and their evolution, highlighting key trends.

The beginnings (2000s)

In the 2000s, AI researchers mainly used general mathematical libraries:

- **NumPy and SciPy**: Providing advanced mathematical functions, they formed the basis for implementing simple models.
- **MATLAB**: Very popular in academic circles, but limited by its high cost and lack of scalability.

These tools required considerable expertise and lacked machine learning-specific features.

The rise of deep learning (2010-2015)

With the advent of deep learning, specialized frameworks have emerged:

- **Theano**: One of the first frameworks to define computational graphs for neural networks.
- **Caffe**: Popular in computer vision, thanks in particular to its efficiency in convolutional networks.

Modern revolutions (2015-2020)

The launch of TensorFlow in 2015 marked a turning point. Developed by Google, it introduced advanced features and exhaustive documentation. PyTorch, launched in 2016 by Facebook, gained in popularity thanks to its flexibility and dynamic approach.

At the same time, cloud platforms such as AWS, Google Cloud AI and Microsoft Azure have democratized access to massive computing power, essential for training complex models.

Integration and democratization (2020-present)

Since the 2020s, AI tools have continued to integrate into everyday workflows thanks to innovations such as :

- **GitHub Copilot**: Using advanced language models to assist developers.
- **ONNX (Open Neural Network Exchange)**: A standard facilitating interoperability between frameworks.

These advances reflect a trend towards simplification and accessibility, while maintaining advanced capabilities for experts.

7.4 Choosing a tool or platform

Choosing an AI tool or platform is a strategic decision that depends on many factors. This section explores the essential criteria and provides practical examples.

Factors to consider

1. **Type of project**
    - Data analysis: Scikit-learn excels in statistical models and classic supervised learning algorithms.
    - Natural language processing (NLP): Hugging Face offers advanced solutions for text-related tasks.
    - Computer vision: PyTorch and TensorFlow are ideal for designing convolutional networks.
2. **Ease of use**

    - Beginner developers: Keras, a high-level API, lets you build models without excessive complexity.
    - Advanced users: PyTorch offers granular control over architectures.
3. **Community support**
    - A tool with an active community guarantees access to educational resources, examples and solutions.
4. **Budget and scale**
    - Cloud platforms: AWS, Azure and Google Cloud offer flexible pricing to suit different budgets.
5. **Interoperability**
    - Standards such as ONNX ensure compatibility between frameworks, facilitating integration in heterogeneous environments.

Case studies

- One startup used Google AutoML to develop a prototype in two weeks, cutting time-to-market in half.
- An industrial company chose PyTorch for its flexibility, enabling complete customization of predictive models.

TensorFlow: Versatile AI leader

TensorFlow, developed by Google Brain, has established itself as a pillar in the field of AI. This section explores its capabilities, its benefits, and a practical tutorial to better understand how it works.

Main features

- **Multi-platform support**: Deployment on servers, browsers (TensorFlow.js) and mobile devices (TensorFlow Lite).

- **Computational graphs**: Static for optimization and dynamic for flexibility.
- **Integrated tools**: TensorBoard for visualization, TensorFlow Hub for pre-trained models.
- **Advanced techniques**: Supports templates such as GPT and GANs for complex tasks.

TensorFlow benefits

1. **Performance**
   - Optimal use of GPUs and TPUs.
2. **Documentation**
   - Comprehensive documentation and official tutorials for all levels.
3. **Interoperability**
   - Compatible with other libraries such as NumPy, Keras and Scikit-learn.

Practical tutorial

A detailed example of training a model on the MNIST dataset is presented in the previous version.

Conclusion

AI tools and platforms are transforming the way projects are conceptualized, developed and deployed. They enable complex technical challenges to be overcome, while making innovation accessible to a wide range of users. By choosing these tools wisely and mastering their capabilities, organizations can not only solve today's problems, but also anticipate tomorrow's challenges. The future of AI rests on these foundations, and investing in their adoption and enhancement is essential.

CHAPTER 8: ROBOTICS AND IA

This chapter explores the integration of artificial intelligence (AI) in robotics, focusing on key aspects such as autonomous navigation, human-robot interaction, collaborative robotics and industrial applications. Through in-depth analysis, we will examine how AI is transforming the capabilities of robots, enabling them to operate more autonomously and efficiently in diverse environments.

8.1 AI integration in robotics

The integration of AI into robotics enables machines to process complex information and make decisions in real time. Thanks to machine learning and natural language processing algorithms, robots can now analyze their environment, learn from experience and adapt to a variety of situations. This synergy between AI and robotics paves the way for innovative applications in many sectors.

AI gives robots extensive perception and decision-making capabilities. For example, systems based on deep neural networks can detect objects, classify images and recognize complex patterns. In addition, AI software platforms embedded in robots enable action scenarios to be simulated and optimized before they are implemented, thereby reducing risk and increasing efficiency. The evolution of reinforcement learning also enables robots to perfect themselves through iterations, demonstrating human-like performance in simulated or real environments.

In addition, interoperability platforms and standardized interfaces enable smoother integration of different software and hardware modules, promoting the development of versatile robots. The growing adoption of AI also explains the growth of robotics markets in areas such as healthcare, logistics and defense, where innovation is crucial to meet changing needs.

8.2 Autonomous navigation

Autonomous navigation is one of the most advanced areas of AI-integrated robotics. Robots equipped with sensors and computer vision algorithms can map their environment and navigate without human intervention. Technologies such as SLAM (Simultaneous Localization and Mapping) enable robots to navigate efficiently in unfamiliar spaces, which is essential for applications ranging from parcel delivery to space exploration.

To guarantee reliable autonomous navigation, several techniques are combined. LiDAR sensors, stereoscopic cameras and radar provide precise data on the immediate environment. This data is then processed by AI algorithms capable of fusing the information to create three-dimensional maps. Path planning algorithms, such as those based on probability graphs or particle swarm optimization, help robots to choose the most efficient routes while avoiding obstacles.

AI in navigation also includes the ability to adapt dynamically. For example, an autonomous robot needs to be able to modify its route if an unexpected obstacle appears or the environment changes. Systems based on supervised or unsupervised learning enable robots to recognize behavioral patterns and anticipate risks, such as the presence of animals or pedestrians.

In industrial sectors, these robots are deployed for tasks such as handling, inspection and surveillance. Fields such as agriculture also benefit from robots with autonomous navigation, capable of harvesting crops or analyzing the health of plantations over vast areas.

8.3 Human-robot interaction

Human-robot interaction is a crucial aspect of AI integration in robotics. Advances in natural language processing and speech recognition enable robots to understand and respond to human commands more intuitively. What's more, robots can be programmed to interpret human emotions, making interactions more natural and effective. This is particularly relevant in contexts such as home assistance or education.

Multimodal interfaces combining speech, gestures and facial expressions greatly enhance human-robot interactions. For example, robots equipped with cameras and depth sensors can detect human movements and respond in a coordinated fashion. Emotional recognition systems, based on the analysis of facial expressions or tone of voice, enable robots to adapt to the emotional state of their interlocutors.

In the healthcare field, these capabilities are being put to good use to provide assistance to elderly patients or those undergoing rehabilitation. Social robots like Pepper or NAO are already being used in hospitals and schools for deliberate and engaging interactions. In addition, work on intelligent exoskeletons uses AI to understand users' motor needs and adjust their movements accordingly.

The challenge remains in resolving misunderstandings and misinterpretations. Researchers are exploring hybrid models combining symbolic knowledge bases and deep learning approaches to improve robots' contextual understanding.

8.4 Collaborative robotics

Collaborative robotics, or cobotics, refers to the use of robots working alongside humans in a shared environment. AI plays an essential role in this dynamic, enabling robots to understand and predict human actions, thus ensuring safe and efficient operations. These collaborative systems are increasingly used on production lines, where they assist workers with repetitive or hazardous tasks.

Cobots are designed with advanced sensors capable of detecting human presence nearby. Deep learning algorithms enable them to understand the gestures and anticipate the intentions of operators. For example, on an assembly line, a cobot can adjust its speed or force according to the actions of the human worker, thus preventing accidents and improving overall efficiency.

Cobots are also equipped with collaborative decision-making mechanisms. They can participate in task planning, identify bottlenecks, and adjust their operation according to the priorities established by their human counterparts. These capabilities reduce downtime and increase the flexibility of industrial processes.

However, integrating cobots into complex environments requires strict standards and extensive testing to ensure compliance with safety regulations. In addition, the training of human operators remains essential to optimize the use of these collaborative tools.

8.5 Industrial applications

The industrial applications of AI-enabled robotics are vast and varied. In the manufacturing industry, intelligent robots optimize production processes, reduce errors and increase productivity. In the logistics sector, autonomous robots manage the storage and distribution of goods. AI also enables predictive maintenance, reducing downtime and improving operational efficiency.

In factories, AI-powered robotic arms perform complex tasks such as the precise assembly of electronic components or the welding of metal structures. Machine learning algorithms detect manufacturing defects at an early stage, reducing the costs associated with non-compliant products. In warehouses, mobile robotics systems like those from Amazon Robotics sort and move parcels with unrivalled precision.

The evolution of digital twins enables companies to simulate their production lines in real time, identifying sticking points and optimizing performance. Autonomous robots, coupled with AI platforms, also monitor equipment to detect anomalies and predict breakdowns before they occur.

In sectors such as oil, underwater robotics are used to inspect and maintain offshore installations. Autonomous drones, meanwhile, carry out surveillance missions in dangerous or inaccessible environments, reducing the risks for human operators.

8.6 Conclusion

In conclusion, the integration of AI into robotics is radically transforming the technological landscape, opening up new possibilities for autonomy, interaction and collaboration. Advances in this field promise to revolutionize not only industry, but also our everyday lives. The future of robotics looks bright, with developments that will set new standards in productivity and innovation.

CHAPTER 9: NATURAL LANGUAGE PROCESSING

This chapter explores the field of natural language processing (NLP), a sub-branch of artificial intelligence that seeks to make computers capable of understanding, interpreting and generating human language in a fluent and natural way. Thanks to impressive advances in fields such as deep learning and language models, NLP is now an integral part of our interaction with technology.

9.1 Language comprehension

Language understanding is one of the most complex tasks in artificial intelligence. It involves enabling a computer system to **understand** the meaning behind human words and sentences. This process requires several advanced techniques and steps:

a) Syntax analysis (or "parsing")

Syntactic analysis is the process of breaking down a sentence to understand its grammatical structure. A syntax tree is often used to visualize the relationship between words in a sentence. For example, the sentence "The cat eats an apple" can be analyzed to identify that "cat" is the subject, "eats" is the verb, and "apple" is the direct object. This structure makes it easy to understand who's doing what and what it relates to.

b) Semantic analysis

Semantic analysis goes beyond syntax, seeking to understand the **meaning of** words in context. For example, the word "bark" could mean the bark of a tree, or the bark of a dog. Modern semantic models use **vector representations** (embeddings), such as the **word embeddings** of Word2Vec or GloVe, to capture the meaning of words through vector spaces.

c) Pragmatic and Contextual Analysis

Pragmatic understanding is the ability to grasp the intentions behind words, which is essential for understanding the context in which a sentence is spoken. A TLN model must therefore integrate the global context to correctly interpret nuances, sarcasm or idiomatic expressions.

For example, the sentence "It's a sunny day, perfect for a walk" might be interpreted differently if spoken after a period of rain or in summer.

d) Pre-trained language models

Models such as **BERT**, **GPT**, or **T5** are powerful language models that are previously trained on huge text corpora to capture linguistic structures and word relationships. These models use **Transformer-type** architectures, which are capable of handling long dependencies in a text, making them more efficient than traditional models such as recurrents (RNN).

9.2 Language generation

Language generation is the art of creating texts that appear natural, coherent and relevant. It requires a **deep understanding of** the subject matter, but also the ability to produce text that respects syntax and grammar.

a) Text generation templates

Generative templates like **GPT-3** or **GPT-4** can create long, complex texts from a few keywords or a prompt. For example, if a template like GPT-3 is given the prompt "Write a short story about a robot and a cat", it can generate a coherent, creative text in a matter of seconds.

b) Language generation applications

There are many areas of application for language generation, including :

- **Automated writing**: Systems can write articles, reports, even poems. Companies use these technologies to produce large-scale content, such as product descriptions or article summaries.
- **Dialogue creation for video games**: In interactive games, dialogs can be dynamically generated according to the player's choices. These dialogs can be adapted to real-time actions and decisions.
- **Code writing**: Tools like **GitHub Copilot**, based on GPT, are used to suggest lines of code based on developer feedback.

c) Quality and consistency control

One of the main difficulties in language generation is maintaining text **coherence**, especially over long sections. Language generation models sometimes tend to lose the thread of conversation or produce unnecessary repetition. Techniques such as **regularization** or **sequence length control mechanisms** are used to avoid these problems.

9.3 Automatic translation

Machine translation is a major application of TLN, enabling texts to be converted from one language to another. Modern systems don't just translate word by word; they understand the **overall meaning of** the text to produce smooth, natural translations.

a) Neural Model-Based Translation

Modern systems use **Recurrent Neural Networks** (RNN) and **Transformers**, which are capable of processing an entire sentence or paragraph before producing the translation. This greatly improves the fluidity and accuracy of translations compared to older systems based on rules or word-by-word translations.

- **For example**, Google Translate now uses **Transformer** models (e.g. **GNMT** - Google Neural Machine Translation) to produce more natural translations, even for complex sentences.

b) Contextual and Specialized Translation

Machine translation is not limited to common languages such as English or Spanish. Systems like **DeepL** or **Amazon Translate** are capable of translating less common and specialized languages, such as technical languages or jargon specific to certain fields (medicine, law, etc.).

9.4 Feeling analysis

Sentiment analysis is a branch of NLT that endeavors to determine the underlying emotion or opinion in a text. It uses **classification techniques** to identify whether a text is positive, negative or neutral.

a) Applications of Feeling Analysis

Sentiment analysis is widely used in several sectors:

- **Marketing and Advertising**: Companies analyze customer feelings about products or services through reviews, opinions and comments on social networks. This enables them to measure **customer satisfaction** and identify opportunities for improvement.
- **Social Media Monitoring**: Organizations monitor public opinion on hot topics or events in real time, analyzing millions of posts on Twitter, Facebook or Instagram.
- **Financial Market Prediction**: Sentiment analysis can be used to predict market movements, by analyzing investors' opinions on specific stocks or global economic events.

b) Feeling Analysis Models

Models such as **VADER** (Valence Aware Dictionary and sEntiment Reasoner) or **BERT** are specially adapted to this task, as they take into account the subtle variations in tone or emotion in texts.

9.5 Chatbots and Virtual Assistants

Chatbots and **virtual assistants** are concrete applications of NLT that interact with users in natural language. These systems are now used in many fields to enhance the user experience and automate certain tasks.

a) Customer service chatbots

Chatbots are widely used to automate **responses to customers** in sectors such as banking, telecommunications or e-commerce. They can answer frequently asked questions, help solve technical problems or provide product information.

b) Virtual Assistants

Assistants like **Siri**, **Google Assistant** and **Alexa** are examples of voice command interfaces that enable users to interact with their devices through voice. These virtual assistants are powered by language processing models that enable them to understand complex requests and perform actions.

c) Personalized interactions

Modern assistants can personalize their responses according to the user's preferences and history. For example, an assistant can remind you of a scheduled appointment, suggest a playlist based on your musical tastes, or even adjust the temperature in your home according to your preferences.

9.6 Conclusion

Natural language processing is a key area of artificial intelligence, profoundly transforming the way we interact with technology. Advances in **machine learning** and **deep learning** now make it possible to process massive volumes of textual data with unprecedented accuracy and efficiency. As the capabilities of TLN develop, we will see increasing adoption of this technology in fields as diverse as healthcare, education, customer service and much more.

CHAPTER 10: IA AND BIG DATA

10.1 Introduction

The era of massive data, supported by rapid technological evolution, has led to an explosion in the volumes of data generated on a daily basis. This transformation is creating new challenges and opportunities for businesses and organizations. In this context, Artificial Intelligence (AI) and Big Data play a central role in enabling these gigantic volumes of information to be processed, analyzed and exploited. This chapter explores the key aspects of this interaction, focusing on data collection, analysis, storage, management and security, while illustrating how these technologies can transform industries and shape the future of business.

10.2 Data Collection

Data collection is the crucial first step in the Big Data analysis process. It involves the acquisition, sorting and recording of data from a variety of sources, to enable its future exploitation. The data collected can be structured, semi-structured or unstructured, requiring methods adapted to each type of data.

Data Sources

- **IoT sensors**: These devices collect real-time data on physical or digital environments. They measure variables such as temperature, pressure, humidity or movement, and enable automatic monitoring and proactive intervention.
- **Social networks**: Facebook, Twitter, LinkedIn, Instagram and other platforms generate constant streams of social data. This data includes posts, interactions, user profiles, and online behavior, which can be used for behavioral analysis, market research or personalized campaigns.
- **Online transactions**: Financial transactions, online purchases, mobile payments and website interaction logs collect a wealth of information on consumer buying habits, preferences and behavior.
- **Information systems**: ERP (Enterprise Resource Planning), CRM, and transactional databases store organizational information such as customer data, inventory, orders or business performance. These data enable more efficient management of resources and relationships.

Collection methods

- **Automated**: Using IoT sensors or automated extraction scripts from databases or web services. This method enables continuous data extraction without human intervention.
- **Semi-automated**: Considering semi-structured or unstructured data (e.g. log files or images), this method may require manual or semi-automated extraction tools before ingestion into databases.
- **Human**: Use of field studies, surveys, questionnaires or interviews, particularly when information is sensitive or specific to the cultural or organizational context.

Problems and challenges

- **Volume**: The massive amount of data collected can outstrip traditional processing capacities.
- **Variety**: Data is often heterogeneous, requiring processing adapted to its nature (text, video, image, audio, etc.).
- **Confidentiality and Regulation**: Compliance with regulations such as RGPD or HIPAA is crucial to protect personal or sensitive data.

10.3 Mass data analysis

Big Data analysis aims to extract meaningful information from colossal volumes of data. Thanks to advanced Artificial Intelligence (AI) algorithms, it becomes possible to interpret this data for prediction, classification or the identification of hidden relationships.

Analysis Techniques

- **Supervised Learning Algorithms**: Used for tasks such as sales prediction, customer service or detection of fraudulent behavior. These models require labeled data and learn complex relationships between variables.
- **Unsupervised learning**: discover structures or groups within data without prior supervision. These techniques are used for customer segmentation or data mining to identify hidden groups or emerging trends.
- **Natural Language Processing (NLP)**: transforms textual data into usable information. This includes semantic analysis, automatic content generation or entity extraction (name, place, etc.).

Tools and Platforms

- **Apache Hadoop**: Distributed system for Big Data processing, capable of managing data sets on multiple machines.
- **TensorFlow**, **PyTorch**: popular frameworks for Deep Learning and advanced data analysis.

Analysis applications

- **Demand forecasting**: Used in the retail sector to adjust inventories or anticipate demand.
- **Sentimental Analysis**: Detects perceptions or attitudes about a brand or product from comments or posts on social networks.
- **Personalization**: Adapting services or products to users' preferences and behaviors.

10.4 Data storage and management

With data growing exponentially, storage and management are becoming major challenges. Traditional solutions such as relational databases are often insufficient to manage the growing variety and volume of data.

Distributed Storage Solutions

- **NoSQL databases**: Optimized for non-relational data. Examples: MongoDB, Cassandra, HBase. These databases offer greater flexibility in terms of schema and parallel processing.
- **Distributed storage**: Solutions such as HDFS or S3 (Amazon) can handle massive volumes while maintaining data resilience and scalability.

Data Management Methods

- **Partitioning** : Spreading data over several servers or machines to improve access speed.
- **Compression**: Reduction of data volume while maintaining data integrity, facilitating data management in distributed systems.

Management Challenges

- **Scalability**: ensure stable performance even as data volumes grow exponentially.
- **Availability**: Guarantee constant accessibility and low latency of data, particularly on distributed architectures.

10.5 Data security

Security is a crucial aspect of Big Data management. The explosion of data poses significant risks in terms of confidentiality and integrity.

Safety mechanisms

- **Data encryption** : Protect data during storage or transfer using robust cryptographic algorithms.
- **Multi-factor authentication**: reinforce access by preventing unauthorized third parties from gaining access.
- **Access Controls**: Manage data access permissions according to specific roles and confidentiality levels.

Cyber threats

- **Data theft**: a growing risk with the evolution of cloud services and the complexity of distributed systems.
- **Ransomware**: Attacks companies via insecure or poorly configured databases.

10.6 Integrating AI and Big Data

The integration of Artificial Intelligence and Big Data can transform massive data into a veritable goldmine of actionable information.

Benefits

- **Process Optimization**: Automate repetitive tasks using predictive models powered by AI algorithms.
- **Advanced Personalization**: The use of Big Data enables the creation of highly personalized user experiences, increasing customer satisfaction and loyalty.

Future prospects

- **Increased accuracy**: Advanced analysis enables more precise predictions and more relevant recommendations.
- **Business model innovation**: New business models based on dynamic data enable us to offer innovative services.

10.7 Conclusion

The interaction between Artificial Intelligence and Big Data is transforming the technological and industrial landscape. By combining advanced analytical capabilities with massive data, organizations can maximize their operational efficiency while discovering new opportunities for growth and innovation. While this interaction raises challenges in terms of data collection, management, security and analysis, it also opens up promising perspectives

CHAPTER 11: RECOMMENDATION SYSTEMS

Recommendation systems play a crucial role in personalizing user experiences on digital platforms such as streaming sites, social networks, e-commerce, and many others. They offer suggestions for articles, films, products or content tailored to users' individual preferences. Using sophisticated algorithms, these systems analyze past behavior and available data to predict what might be relevant to each user.

1. Collaborative Filtering

Collaborative filtering is a widely used method for generating recommendations. It is based on the idea that user behaviors can be compared to predict future preferences. Here are the two main sub-categories of collaborative filtering:

a. User-based collaborative filtering

In this type, the system compares users with each other, drawing on their interaction histories to make recommendations. If two users have similar behaviors (i.e. similar tastes for a certain number of items or content), then the system suggests items similar to those enjoyed by the first user.

- **Example**: If User A has watched several science fiction films, and User B has shown similar interests (by also watching similar films or positively rating films in the same genre), the system will recommend science fiction films to both users.

Advantages :

- Adapted to new interactions without requiring additional item information.
- Reliable for recommending new content when user data is abundant.

Disadvantages :

- **Cold start** problem: Difficulty in providing relevant recommendations for new users or new content, due to lack of historical data on user preferences.
- Risk of **overfitting**: By focusing solely on past behavior, the system can become too rigid and fail to capture broader preferences.

b. Article-based collaborative filtering

This type focuses on comparing items or elements themselves based on the users who have enjoyed them. This makes it possible to offer recommendations based on the relationships between items rather than on users.

- **Example**: A user who has liked a specific product may receive recommendations for similar products (identical or close in attributes) that have also been liked by other users with similar interests.

Advantages :

- Less prone to cold-start problems, as it's based on past user interactions on similar items.
- Avoids the social biases that can affect user-based collaborative filtering.

Disadvantages :

- Limitation in the diversification of recommendations: based on similarities between items, which may not capture all user preferences.

2. Content-based Filtering

Content-based filtering focuses on the intrinsic characteristics of items (articles, films, products). This method takes specific information about recommended items, such as their description, genre, keywords, or detailed features, and compares it with the user's preferences.

Process :

- **Feature extraction**: The system extracts attributes such as genres, tags or keywords from a film or product.
- **Comparison**: Similar items are then recommended based on these attributes.
- **Example**: If a user likes horror films with a mysterious atmosphere and paranormal themes, the system will recommend other films with similar characteristics (same genre, similar themes, etc.).

Advantages :

- Simple and explicit: The system is based on well-defined rules and measurable characteristics.
- Adapted to new content: Whether the user is new or not, the system can always recommend similar items based on existing characteristics.

Disadvantages :

- Lack of diversity: Does not take into account social preferences or those of other users.
- Less effective with more complex content or less explicit interactions.

3. Hybrid Methods

Hybrid methods combine the advantages of collaborative and content-based approaches to generate more accurate and diverse recommendations. These systems exploit the strengths of both methods while limiting their respective weaknesses.

a. Similar hybrid filtering

This type combines collaborative and content-based methods for improved performance. The system uses **all user information as** well as **item attributes** to make more accurate recommendations.

- **Example**: A user who has watched action movies and liked some of them will receive recommendations based on both similar past behavior (collaborative) and the characteristics of the movies liked (content-based).

Advantages :

- Improved accuracy of recommendations.
- Reduced bias compared to a single method.

Disadvantages :

- Increased complexity in managing different sources of information.
- Higher computational cost.

b. Combined hybrid filtering

In this case, the two methods are used independently, then their results are combined to offer better customization.

- **Example**: When a user interacts with a platform, recommendations are generated separately using collaborative and content-based methods. The two results are then merged to produce a final suggestion.

4. Challenges and prospects

Despite significant progress in the field of recommender systems, several challenges remain:

- **Diversity of recommendations**: Maintaining sufficient diversity while offering personalized suggestions remains a complex task, as users can quickly tire of the same types of recommendations.
- **Privacy**: The massive use of user data raises ethical concerns about data security and confidentiality. It is crucial to protect this information without compromising the quality of recommendations.
- **Interpretability of algorithms**: Users and even companies sometimes find it difficult to understand how algorithms arrive at their recommendations. This limits their acceptability and adoption in critical contexts.

Future prospects

As technologies evolve, recommender systems will need to adapt to rapid change. Systems will need to integrate methods based on artificial intelligence and machine learning to deliver even more personalized and relevant user experiences. In addition, the integration of technologies such as natural language processing (NLP) and computer vision will open up interesting prospects for richer, more diversified recommendations.

CHAPTER 12: SAFETY AND IA

This chapter takes a closer look at the crucial aspects of safety in the field of artificial intelligence (AI). AI, as an evolving technology, brings many opportunities, but also significant security challenges. With increased use in critical areas such as healthcare, finance, national security, and many others, it is essential to understand the potential risks and possible solutions to ensure optimal security.

1. AI system safety

The importance of safety in AI systems

The security of AI systems has become a fundamental issue in a world where these technologies increasingly influence the strategic and operational decisions of organizations. AI systems handling sensitive data need to be protected against threats such as malicious manipulation, data leakage, and decision errors.

Key issues :

1. **Unauthorized access** :
    - AI is often based on complex models and algorithms that need to be protected from unauthorized access.
    - This includes the use of mechanisms such as multi-factor authentication (MFA), role-based access control (RBAC), and intrusion detection.
2. **Model Integrity** :
    - AI models are vulnerable to manipulation of their training data, which can lead to erroneous predictions and unreliable decisions.
    - Regular auditing and monitoring of AI models helps to identify these vulnerabilities.

2. AI for Cybersecurity

The role of AI in Cybersecurity

AI is a valuable tool for strengthening cybersecurity, enabling rapid and effective detection of threats, while automating responses.

1. **Detection of Abnormal Behavior** :

  - AI analyzes network and user data to detect anomalies, such as intrusions or suspicious activity.
  - For example, a bank can use AI systems to monitor transactions in real time and flag up suspicious activity.
2. **Automated Responses** :
  - In the event of incidents, AI systems can automate the taking of preventive measures, such as immediately blocking a malicious IP address or temporarily disabling a compromised account.
3. **Using Machine Learning** :
  - Machine learning enables AI systems to improve their ability to detect ever-changing threat patterns, making solutions more responsive to modern attacks.

3. Adversarial attacks

Defining Adversarial Attacks

Adversarial attacks are designed to disrupt the proper functioning of AI systems by subtly manipulating their inputs. These sophisticated techniques present a major challenge to the security of AI systems, as they often exploit existing vulnerabilities in data processing.

1. **Types of Adversarial Attacks** :
  - **Input modification**: For example, a slight modification of an image intended for a facial recognition system may result in an error in correct identification.
  - **Trap attack**: Substitution of test data with falsified data to deceive the AI model about its real performance.
2. **Defense Techniques** :
  - **Disturbance detection** : Development of robust methods for detecting disturbances introduced into inputs.
  - **Robustness testing**: using simulations to test model response to adversarial attacks.

4. Fraud detection

AI and Fraud Detection

Fraud detection using AI helps minimize financial losses by identifying abnormal behavior in transactions, logins, or other interactions.

1. **Machine learning** :
    - AI uses algorithms to analyze thousands of transactions to isolate suspicious behavior, such as unusual amounts or repetitive patterns consistent with fraudulent activity.
2. **Customization and adaptation** :
    - AI systems can be trained on new types of fraud and adapt to constantly evolving fraud methods thanks to supervised and unsupervised learning models.

5. Privacy Policy

Security of Personal Data

The protection of personal data is crucial, especially in the age of automated processing of sensitive information, where breaches can have serious impacts on privacy.

1. **Sensitive Data Management** :
    - AI helps to identify and classify sensitive data according to its level of risk, enabling appropriate measures to be taken for its security.
2. **Security techniques** :
    - **Anonymization**: Remove personal information while retaining relevant data for analysis.
    - **Encryption**: Ensure that personal data remains secure using advanced cryptographic algorithms.

6. Conclusion

Security and artificial intelligence are intimately linked in a world where AI systems are increasingly ubiquitous. Security challenges, such as adversarial attacks and data breaches, require technology solutions and rigorous approaches to ensure the confidentiality, integrity and resilience of AI systems. Organizations need to take a proactive and continuous approach to ensuring system and data security.

CHAPTER 13: IA IN VIDEO GAMES

This chapter takes an in-depth look at the evolution of artificial intelligence (AI) in video games, highlighting its history, its various applications for non-player characters (NPCs), performance optimization, procedural content generation, as well as its integration into virtual reality. AI has considerably transformed the gaming experience, making interactions more immersive, dynamic and realistic.

1. History of AI in games

AI in video games dates back to the 1950s and 1960s, with simple games such as **"Tennis for Two"** and **"Spacewar!"**, where AI handled basic elements such as the simulation of simple movements. However, it was only as technology advanced, notably with the evolution of consoles and computer systems, that AI began to become more complex.

80s: AI took its first serious steps with systems based on predictable patterns. **"Pac-Man"**, for example, used enemies that followed fixed paths and did not evolve according to the player's behavior.

90s: With the introduction of the first 3D consoles like the PlayStation and the evolution of computers, AI algorithms were able to incorporate more complex behaviors such as real-time decision-making and a greater ability to adapt to the player's actions. **"Quake"**, **"Doom"** and **"Resident Evil 2"** all use AI systems that take into account the player's tactics and adjust their behavior accordingly.

2. AI for non-player characters (NPCs)

NPCs are essential for creating lively, interactive game worlds. With AI, they can react more realistically and naturally, enhancing the overall player experience.

a. Decision trees

Decision trees are logical structures used to guide NPC actions in specific scenarios. These systems enable characters to adopt intelligent, context-sensitive behaviors, such as appropriate responses to specific situations or in-game stimuli. For example, in **"The Elder Scrolls V: Skyrim"**, NPCs react to various actions such as the threat of combat or exploration of the environment.

b. Behavioral systems

These systems use algorithms to define action routines based on perceived stimuli. In **"Grand Theft Auto"**, NPCs interact not only with the player but also with each other and the environment, creating a dynamic atmosphere where realistic behaviors emerge naturally.

c. Machine learning

Artificial intelligence using deep learning algorithms enables NPCs to improve their abilities by learning from players' past actions. **"Detroit: Become Human"** is an example where NPCs learn to respond more realistically and emotionally according to the player's choices, making each interaction unique and engaging.

3. Performance optimization

With game worlds constantly evolving, performance is a crucial element in guaranteeing an immersive, uninterrupted experience.

a. Culling and visual optimization

Culling is a technique in which the AI excludes non-visible objects or elements, considerably reducing the graphics card's workload. This allows for larger worlds without sacrificing fluidity. For example, in **"Assassin's Creed Odyssey"**, the AI dynamically optimizes what is rendered in the background to minimize performance losses.

b. Level of Detail (LOD)

LOD adjusts the visual complexity of an object or environment according to its distance from the player. This technique, commonly used in games such as **"The Witcher 3"** or **"Cyberpunk 2077"**, helps maintain optimal performance while maintaining high visual quality when the player is close to objects.

c. Workload balancing

AI also helps spread the load between CPU and GPU for a lag-free experience. This is essential in competitive multiplayer games where low latency is crucial.

4. Procedural generation

Procedural generation uses algorithms to create content automatically, reducing developers' workload while offering an infinite variety of content.

a. Levels and environments

In games like **"No Man's Sky"**, AI procedurally generates planets, terrains and structures. Each exploration is unique, thanks to algorithms that ensure the content is diverse and engaging.

b. Dynamic quests and stories

Procedural quests, like those used in **"The Elder Scrolls Online"**, generate unique missions for each game session. This keeps players interested with fresh, unexpected content.

5. Virtual Reality (VR) and AI

The integration of AI into virtual reality opens up a new dimension of immersion and personalization.

a. Adaptive interactions

The AI analyzes the player's movements in real time, adjusting behavior and gameplay according to the player's actions and choices. In experiences such as **"Half-Life: Alyx"**, enemies, interactive objects and even environments react realistically to the player's movements.

b. immersive experiences

AI in VR makes interaction much more natural. Adaptive systems analyze every action, even micro-movements, to deliver an experience perfectly tailored to each user. For example, in **"Beat Saber VR"**, enemies adjust to the player's movements to provide personalized challenges.

6. Conclusion

Artificial intelligence has profoundly transformed the field of video games, offering more dynamic, immersive and adaptive experiences. Its ongoing evolution, in synergy with cutting-edge technologies such as VR and procedural generation, promises even broader horizons for developers and gamers alike, with greater personalization and depth in digital interactions. AI remains at the heart of videogame innovation, constantly redefining the limits of what's possible in virtual worlds.

CHAPTER 14: IA AND THE ENVIRONMENT

This chapter delves deeper into the interconnection between artificial intelligence (AI) and today's environmental challenges. By exploring various areas such as resource management, environmental monitoring, climate resilience, sustainable design and renewable energy optimization, we discover how AI is contributing to a more sustainable and balanced future. Here's a detailed exploration of each aspect:

1. AI for Resource Management

Artificial intelligence helps optimize the use of natural resources, guaranteeing sustainable management of raw materials, water and agricultural soils.

a. Optimizing water use

- **Irrigation Needs Prediction**
  AI uses weather data, soil surveys and crop information to anticipate irrigation requirements. Thanks to predictive models, it is possible to reduce water wastage while maintaining optimum yields.
  Example: AI algorithms integrated into sensor systems enable precise irrigation, saving water and improving agricultural performance.
- **Aquifer Resource Management**
  Using advanced machine learning technologies, AI detects the risks of overexploitation of groundwater resources and helps to establish sustainable management strategies.
  Example: predictive models analyze historical and current data on water levels to prevent shortages and optimize the use of water resources.

b. Soil and agricultural optimization

- **Soil Analysis**
  Artificial intelligence enables in-depth analysis of the chemical and biological composition of soils. This approach enables optimal management of agricultural soils, limiting the use of chemical fertilizers while maintaining high productivity.
  Example: AI helps identify areas requiring specific intervention, reducing environmental impact while improving soil quality.

- **Agricultural yield prediction**
  Thanks to statistical and predictive models, AI anticipates climatic variations and their impact on harvests, offering solutions adapted to agricultural challenges.

c. Raw materials management

- **Natural Resource Detection**
  AI helps map and monitor stocks of scarce resources such as precious metals or strategic minerals, offering sustainable management and efficient exploitation.
  Example: AI algorithms monitor geographical data to predict the depletion of natural resources and propose sustainable alternatives.

2. Environmental Monitoring

Real-time environmental monitoring is essential for identifying environmental problems and taking immediate action.

a. AI-enabled sensors and drones

- **Real-time data collection**
  Sensors equipped with artificial intelligence analyze data from various environmental parameters such as air, water and soil quality. This data enables rapid detection of pollution sources or ecological threats.
  Example: Autonomous drones equipped with AI sensors carry out environmental monitoring missions, even in areas inaccessible to man.
- **Automatic Pollution Analysis**
  AI enables rapid identification of pollution using image recognition and natural language processing models, facilitating immediate response.

b. Satellite image analysis

- **Deforestation detection**
  Artificial intelligence analyzes satellite images to track deforestation and changes in land use on a large scale. These analyses enable proactive management of ecologically sensitive

areas.
Example: AI models distinguish areas affected by deforestation and alert authorities to major environmental changes.

- **Species and habitat monitoring** Thanks to advanced AI systems, the monitoring of animal migrations and natural habitats is automated, facilitating conservation efforts.

3. Climate resilience

In the face of climate change, AI is becoming indispensable for strengthening the resilience of ecosystems and communities.

a. Climate risk modeling

- **Climate forecasting** Artificial intelligence analyzes massive sets of climate data to predict phenomena such as floods, droughts or storms, enabling better planning and risk management. **Example**: Predictive simulations help plan infrastructures adapted to extreme weather conditions.
- **Climate Data Management** AI algorithms process a variety of data, from historical weather records to future climate projections, helping to anticipate the impacts of climate change.

b. Resilience solutions

- **Adaptation planning** AI supports the creation of adaptation strategies, analyzing complex scenarios and providing optimized solutions for various climate risks.
  Example: AI models help build resilience strategies for coastal areas threatened by sea-level rise.

4. Sustainable design

AI guides the design of greener, more environmentally-friendly spaces and infrastructures.

a. Optimizing sustainable buildings

- **Energy-efficient design**
  AI helps design buildings that are optimized for energy consumption, integrating eco-friendly materials and intelligent automation systems to maximize their environmental sustainability.
  Example: AI platforms assess a building's energy performance in real time, optimizing the use of resources and reducing its carbon footprint.
- **Materials simulation**
  AI algorithms test sustainable material combinations to assess their environmental impact throughout their lifecycle.

b. Sustainable urban development

- **Improving urban infrastructure**
  AI helps to simulate sustainable urban models, enabling optimal management of public spaces while integrating ecological solutions such as natural parks or green spaces.

5. Renewable energy and AI

The efficient integration of renewable energies into power grids thanks to AI is crucial to the energy transition.

a. Smart Grid management

- **Generation and Distribution Optimization**
  AI maximizes the integration of renewable energies into power grids by dynamically adjusting demand and supply, minimizing losses and increasing energy efficiency.
  Example: AI anticipates consumption peaks and adjusts electricity production accordingly, guaranteeing optimal use of resources.

b. Microgrid management

- **Local Grid Management**
  Microgrids managed by AI ensure local management of energy resources, enabling better adaptation to fluctuations in renewable energy production.
  Example: AI optimizes the management of batteries and energy

storage systems in microgrids, guaranteeing constant energy production.

Conclusion

Artificial intelligence offers innovative and complex solutions to today's environmental challenges. From natural resource management and environmental monitoring to sustainable design and renewable energy optimization, AI plays a central role in creating a sustainable and resilient future. By integrating these technologies in various sectors, it is possible to build a balanced ecosystem that respects natural resources.

CHAPTER 15: THE FUTURE OF ARTIFICIAL INTELLIGENCE

This chapter explores the future prospects of artificial intelligence (AI), focusing on emerging technological trends, the development of general AI, the impact of AI on society, human-machine collaborations, and future innovations. Through this analysis, we will attempt to understand how AI could transform various aspects of our daily and professional lives in the years to come.

Introduction

Artificial intelligence (AI) is redefining the boundaries of what is possible in diverse fields, such as healthcare, education, finance, security and transportation. With rapid technological advances, AI continues to evolve towards more complex, adaptive and autonomous applications. However, this development raises important questions in terms of ethics, regulation and liability. This chapter explores the many dimensions of AI and its potential long-term impact on society and the economy.

Technology Trends

AI technologies are advancing at an impressive pace, offering ever more tailored solutions to today's complex needs. Here are the main technological trends to consider:

1. Deep Learning

Deep learning is the cornerstone of modern artificial intelligence applications. This technology enables artificial neural networks to simulate complex human cognitive processes:

- **Increasingly deep models** : Deep neural networks, such as Transformer architectures and convolutional networks, are capable of processing huge volumes of data, offering superior performance in areas such as image recognition, language detection and predictive analysis.
- **Self-learning**: Models are designed to continually improve with experience, reducing the need for intensive human supervision.

2. Natural Language Processing (NLP)

Natural language processing is evolving exponentially, enabling much more natural interactions between machines and users. Applications include :

- **Language Synthesis**: Automatic generation of written or spoken content from complex text descriptions or queries.
- **Contextual Analysis**: Ability to understand nuances in language, facilitating more natural and relevant interactions.

3. Computer Vision and Object Recognition

Computer vision systems are becoming increasingly sophisticated, with a wide range of applications in sectors such as surveillance, industrial robotics and medicine:

- **Object Detection**: Use advanced models to analyze images in real time and identify objects or situations, essential for logistics management or security.
- **Improving Autonomous Systems**: AI in computer vision enables autonomous vehicles and drones to interact more safely with their environment.

4. Quantum AI and Big Data

With the rise of quantum technologies and Big Data processing capabilities, AI continues to push back the boundaries of what's possible:

- **Quantum AI**: Artificial intelligence combined with quantum computing power could unlock radical innovations in fields such as cryptography, complex chemical simulations and drug discovery.
- **Massive Data Management**: The analysis of large quantities of data, in real or near-real time, enables better decision-making in the financial, predictive medicine and business intelligence sectors.

General AI development (AGI)

The ultimate goal of General Artificial Intelligence (GAI) remains an ambitious but complex dream. Unlike specialized AI, AGI aspires to imitate human intelligence in all its dimensions:

1. Progress and challenges

- **Future ambitions**: Although specialized AI is reaching impressive levels, AGI must overcome major challenges, such as generalizing learning across a multitude of domains and replicating human cognitive flexibility.

- **Ethical and philosophical context**: The development of an AGI system raises fundamental questions about consciousness, control and the ethical limits of autonomous systems capable of complex strategic decisions.

2. Potential applications

- **Superintelligence**: Although still a long way off, AGI could potentially surpass human intelligence in a variety of fields, from science to art to interpersonal relations.
- **Societal impact**: The ethical and societal implications are enormous, requiring international regulation and rigorous control standards to avoid abuses.

AI's impact on society

The impact of artificial intelligence on society is both enriching and worrying:

1. Social benefits

- **Information access**: AI is transforming the way information is processed and disseminated, making access systems more democratic and personalized.
- **Optimizing public services**: AI-driven automation enables more efficient and equitable management of public services, particularly in healthcare, education and public safety management.
- **Job creation**: Although some professions are threatened by automation, new jobs are emerging in fields linked to supervision, ethical management and the development of advanced algorithms.

2. Social challenges

- **Privacy and security**: Massive data collection and analysis are generating growing concerns about the privacy and security of personal data.

- **Technological inequalities**: The rapid adoption of AI could exacerbate technological gaps between populations with access to technology and those who are excluded, leading to a digital divide.

Man-Machine collaborations

Collaboration between humans and machines makes it possible to exploit the strengths of both, resulting in optimized solutions in a number of sectors:

1. Health & Medical

- **Diagnostic assistance**: AI helps doctors diagnose complex conditions faster and more accurately.
- **Assisted Surgery**: AI systems offer real-time assistance during surgical procedures, increasing precision and reducing risk.

2. Legal and Financial Sectors

- **Automated Audit**: In legal and financial services, AI algorithms facilitate automatic document verification and financial risk management.

Foresight and Innovation

The future of AI lies in a forward-looking vision that integrates sustainable and ethical solutions to meet societal needs:

1. Responsible Innovation

- **Sustainable development**: Future innovations must take into account ethical and environmental aspects, with reduced carbon impacts and transparent development practices.
- **Multi-sector collaboration**: AI development requires cooperation between governments, researchers, private companies and international institutions for effective management.

2. Industries of the Future

- **AI in Healthcare and Education**: The emergence of AI solutions for personalized education and predictive medicine will define the next stages of innovation.

Conclusion

Artificial intelligence has the potential to radically transform our society and lifestyles. However, to ensure an inclusive and equitable future, ethical precautions, robust regulations and international collaboration are essential. AI must be seen as an opportunity, not only technological but also social, capable of improving our daily lives while respecting the fundamental principles of respect for rights and transparency.

CHAPTER 16: INTELLECTUAL PROPERTY

Intellectual Property: A Pillar of Innovation and Creativity

What is Intellectual Property (IP)?

Intellectual property (IP) is a legal field that protects the creations of the human mind. It encompasses a set of rights that guarantee creators, inventors and artists recognition and protection of their works against unauthorized use by third parties. These rights cover a variety of creations, from technical inventions to literary and artistic works, trademarks and industrial designs. By providing such protection, IP contributes not only to the recognition of creators, but also to overall economic development.

The Two Main Categories of Intellectual Property

Intellectual property falls into two main categories: industrial property and copyright. Each of these categories offers specific protection for different types of creations, while meeting the distinct needs of creators and businesses.

1. Industrial property

Industrial property concerns the technical and commercial aspects of intellectual creations, including inventions, trademarks and industrial designs. The main aim of this branch is to encourage innovation and protect the rights of rights holders against counterfeiting or usurpation.

a) Patents

Patents are exclusive rights that protect technical inventions. They allow an inventor to exploit his or her innovation without the risk of being copied by third parties for a limited period, generally 20 years. To be eligible for a patent, an invention must be new, inventive and capable of industrial application. This system encourages technological innovation by providing a legal framework that guarantees economic rewards for efforts devoted to research and development.

Patents cover a wide range of inventions, from manufacturing processes to electronic devices, medical treatment methods and software engineering innovations. Creators thus benefit from a temporary monopoly, enabling them to make their research and development efforts profitable.

b) Brands

Trademarks protect distinctive signs such as names, logos, symbols and other visual or sound elements that differentiate a company's products or services. They enable consumers to easily recognize a company's products or services from those of its competitors.

Brands play an essential role in branding and the creation of a strong brand image. They ensure immediate recognition of products or services, while creating intangible commercial value. Companies can benefit from effective brand protection against usurpation or unauthorized use of their visual identities.

c) Designs

Designs protect the aesthetic appearance of products. They cover aspects such as a product's unique shapes, patterns, colors and textures. This form of industrial property prevents unauthorized copying of a specific design. Designers can use design rights to ensure that their work is unique and distinctive in the marketplace.

Design rights play an essential role in the design industry, ensuring that product designers do not see their work counterfeited or imitated by competitors.

2. Copyright

Copyright protects literary and artistic works, including books, music, film, painting, photography, theater and more. Unlike industrial property, copyright does not require registration to be recognized. However, it is advisable to register your works for reasons of proof and legal certainty.

Copyright grants creators exclusive rights over the exploitation of their works, enabling them to control the use, distribution and dissemination of their creations. This form of intellectual property is essential to ensure that artists and writers can profit financially from their works.

a) Protection of literary and artistic works

Copyright protects not only works in their material form, but also their creative content. This includes elements such as ideas, emotions and concepts, as well as their expression through various means, such as language, music or visual forms.

Works protected by copyright include :

- **Books**: Novels, poetry, essays, articles, etc.
- **Music**: composition, arrangements, lyrics, audio or video recordings.
- **Films**: Short films, feature films, documentaries, audiovisual works.
- **Works of art**: paintings, sculptures, photographs, illustrations, etc.

Creators have the exclusive right to authorize or refuse reproduction, distribution or adaptation of their works.

b) Duration of protection

Copyright offers protection to the creator for the duration of his or her life, plus a fixed period that varies from country to country. In Europe, for example, copyright generally extends until 70 years after the death of the author. This enables artists, writers and other creators to receive income from their works for several decades.

Importance of Intellectual Property

Intellectual property is of fundamental importance to many aspects of economic, cultural and social development. It guarantees rights for creators, while stimulating innovation and competition in the marketplace. Here are the main reasons for its importance:

1. Encouraging innovation

Intellectual property is essential for stimulating innovation and creativity. By providing legal protection, it encourages inventors and creators to invest time and resources in developing new ideas. Thanks to this guarantee, innovators can test concepts without fear of being copied or exploited by others without their consent.

Patents, for example, encourage scientific research and development by providing a framework that rewards innovation with temporary, exclusive protection. This enables inventors to develop technologies before they become available to the public.

2. Protecting creators' rights

Intellectual property ensures that creators can benefit from the fruits of their labor. This protection is crucial, as it ensures that the efforts and investments made in creation are fairly compensated. Without IP, many artists, writers, inventors and businesses could easily face infringement of their rights, reducing their motivation to produce original works.

3. Economic Development

IP plays a key role in stimulating economic growth by supporting innovation and promoting competition in the marketplace. Companies that own IP rights often enjoy a competitive advantage, as they can protect their products and services against copying or counterfeiting. This encourages the creation of value and the marketing of new products and services.

Challenges of Intellectual Property

Despite its crucial role in protecting rights, intellectual property faces a number of challenges in a globalized and technologically advanced world. These challenges need to be addressed to ensure effective and equitable protection of rights.

1. Piracy and counterfeiting

The advent of digital technology has facilitated the unauthorized reproduction of content, leading to a massive increase in piracy and copyright infringement. Product counterfeiting, illegal access to software and the downloading of protected content without consent have considerable financial impacts on creators and businesses alike.

Digital technologies enable easy distribution of protected content, making it difficult to detect infringements and enforce rights.

2. Market globalization

Globalization complicates the protection of IP rights on an international scale. Each country has its own IP regulations and systems, making it difficult to enforce rights uniformly in global markets. Multinational companies often have to juggle separate legislation, making the management and enforcement of rights much more complex.

3. The emergence of advanced technologies

New technologies, such as artificial intelligence, blockchain and the Internet of Things (IoT), raise important questions about rights ownership and the protection of works generated or manipulated by intelligent machines. This calls for constant adaptation of IP laws to meet the challenges posed by these innovations.

Conclusion

Intellectual property is a fundamental pillar of economic, cultural and technological development. It protects the rights of creators while stimulating innovation and creativity. However, with modern challenges such as piracy, globalization and technological advances, it is crucial to adjust and evolve to ensure effective protection of rights in a constantly changing world.

GENERAL CONCLUSION

Artificial intelligence (AI) has transcended its status as a purely technical tool to become a driving force capable of redefining the foundations of our society. Over the course of the chapters, we have explored its evolution, its fundamental principles, its multiple applications and its ethical, legal and environmental implications. This exploration has highlighted that AI is much more than a simple technological advance: it embodies a global transformation that affects economic, social and cultural domains.

1. A multidimensional transformation

AI is at the heart of strategic sectors, from healthcare and education to finance, industry and the environment. It has enabled spectacular progress:

In the medical field, it improves early diagnosis, personalizes treatment and contributes to drug discovery.

In the environmental field, she optimizes the management of natural resources, monitors ecosystems and promotes sustainable practices.

In information and communication systems, it simplifies man-machine interaction, while offering personalized recommendations that influence our daily choices.

However, this transformation goes beyond technical improvements. It is redefining our traditional conceptions of work, creativity and autonomy, while at the same time challenging existing economic and social structures.

2. The challenges ahead

Despite its many promises, AI raises complex challenges that must be overcome:

Algorithmic biases: AI, trained on biased data, can reproduce or amplify discrimination. This poses a major problem, particularly in sensitive areas such as recruitment, justice and facial recognition.

Ethics and privacy: AI relies on massive volumes of personal data, raising concerns about privacy and the misuse of this information.

Accountability and transparency: AI systems, often described as "black boxes", sometimes lack transparency in their decision-making, making it difficult to apportion responsibility in the event of error or harm.

Environmental impact: The training of AI models, especially large-scale ones, consumes considerable amounts of energy, which means we need to think about more sustainable approaches.

3. Opportunities for a better future

For AI to become a real lever for progress, a proactive and collaborative approach is needed:

Appropriate regulations: Developing legal frameworks that encourage innovation while protecting the rights of individuals is essential. This includes laws on data use, algorithmic liability and intellectual property of AI-generated works.

Inclusion and diversity: Encouraging diverse participation in AI development will reduce bias and better meet the needs of a global society.

Interdisciplinary research: Combining the technical sciences with disciplines such as philosophy, law and sociology is crucial to anticipating the long-term impacts of AI.

4. The future of artificial intelligence

AI will continue to expand in unexpected directions. Emerging technologies such as General Artificial Intelligence (GAI) could one day rival human intelligence in a wide range of tasks. In other news:

Emotional AI systems could transform the way we interact with machines, making them more intuitive and responsive to our needs.

In education, AI could democratize access to knowledge and provide personalized solutions on a large scale.

Autonomous and collaborative robotics will make it possible to explore previously inaccessible territories, while reshaping industrial and domestic environments.

5. A collective responsibility

As a company, we have a responsibility to shape this technological revolution so that it reflects our values and aspirations. This involves a delicate balance:

Exploit the opportunities offered by AI while limiting its risks.

Ensure that its benefits are distributed equitably, reducing rather than exacerbating inequalities.

Promote ethical and inclusive governance that protects fundamental rights while encouraging innovation.

Artificial intelligence is at a crossroads: it can drive a prosperous and inclusive future or, on the contrary, exacerbate divisions and inequalities if mismanaged. The key lies in a balanced approach, guided by ethical principles and a long-term vision.

Ultimately, AI is not just a technological tool, but a reflection of our choices as humanity. By learning to understand it, control it and use it responsibly, we have a unique opportunity to build a world where technology and humanity progress hand in hand.

REFERENCES

Books

[1]. Russell, S., & Norvig, P. (2021). Artificial Intelligence: A Modern Approach (4e edition). Pearson Education.

[2]. Goodfellow, I., Bengio, Y., & Courville, A. (2016). Deep Learning. MIT Press.

[3]. Domingos, P. (2015). The Master Algorithm: How the Quest for the Ultimate Learning Machine Will Remake Our World. Basic Books.

[4]. Chollet, F. (2018). Deep Learning with Python. Manning Publications.

[5]. Bostrom, N. (2014). Superintelligence: Paths, Dangers, Strategies. Oxford University Press.

Academic articles

[6]. LeCun, Y., Bengio, Y., & Hinton, G. (2015). Deep Learning. Nature, 521(7553), 436-444.

[7]. Silver, D., Schrittwieser, J., Simonyan, K., et al. (2017). Mastering the Game of Go Without Human Knowledge. Nature, 550(7676), 354-359.

[8]. Vaswani, A., Shazeer, N., Parmar, N., et al. (2017). Attention Is All You Need. Advances in Neural Information Processing Systems (NeurIPS).

[9]. Lake, B. M., Ullman, T. D., Tenenbaum, J. B., & Gershman, S. J. (2017). Building Machines That Learn and Think Like People. Behavioral and Brain Sciences, 40, e253.

[10]. Zhang, X., Zhao, J., & LeCun, Y. (2015). Text Understanding from Scratch. arXiv preprint arXiv:1502.01710.

[11]. Technical Reports and Documents

[12]. European Commission. (2020). Ethics Guidelines for Trustworthy AI.

[13]. World Economic Forum. (2021). The Future of Jobs Report.

[14]. McKinsey & Company (2022). The State of AI in 2022: Progress, Trends, and Challenges.

[15]. OpenAI. (2023). GPT-4 Technical Report.

[16]. IEEE Global Initiative. (2019). Ethically Aligned Design: A Vision for Prioritizing Human Well-being with Autonomous and Intelligent Systems.

Practical Applications and Case Studies

[17]. Ng, A. (2018). AI Transformation Playbook. Landing AI.

[18]. Google AI (2020). Responsible AI Practices.

[19]. IBM Research (2021). AI Fairness 360: Understanding Bias in AI Models.

[20]. Tesla (2022). Advancements in Autonomous Driving with AI.

[21]. Microsoft AI. (2023). AI and Sustainability: Leveraging Technology for Environmental Impact.

[22]. Kaggle (2024). Datasets and Competitions for Machine Learning and AI. Available at: https://www.kaggle.com.

[23]. TensorFlow Blog (2023). AI Models and Innovations. Available at: https://blog.tensorflow.org.

[24]. OpenAI Blog (2023). Developments in Large Language Models. Available at: https://openai.com/blog.

[25]. Medium: Towards Data Science (2023). Exploring AI Algorithms. Available at: https://towardsdatascience.com.

[26]. Coursera. (2024). AI for Everyone by Andrew Ng. Available at: https://www.coursera.org.

MIX
Papier aus verantwortungsvollen Quellen
Paper from responsible sources
FSC® C105338

Printed by Books on Demand GmbH, Norderstedt / Germany